MW00568619

Winning

Ways

Vol. 2: More of The Right Stuff

Success in South Central Ontario

Michael B. Davie

Manor House Publishing Inc.

National Library of Canada
Cataloguing in Publication Data:

Davie, Michael B., 1954-
Winning Ways / Michael B. Davie.

Includes bibliographical references.
Contents: v. 1. The Right Stuff – v. 2. More Of The Right
Stuff: Success In South Central Ontario.

ISBN 0-9731956-2-2 (v.1) – ISBN 0-9731956-5-7 (v.2)

    1.   Businesspeople – Canada – Biography.
       I. Title.
       II. Title: The Right Stuff.
       III. Title: More of The Right Stuff

HC112.5.A2D39 2002   338.092'271   C2002-905153-3

Copyright 2003-10-15 by Michael B. Davie.
Published November 15, 2003
by Manor House Publishing Inc.
(905) 648-2193 www.manor-house.biz.

Printed in Canada by Webcom Limited.
First edition. 224 pages. All rights reserved by author.
Book concept/cover design: Michael B. Davie.
The publisher gratefully acknowledges the financial support
of the Book Publishing Industry Development Program
(BPIDP), Department of Canadian Heritage.

Acknowledgements

As always, this book would not have been possible without the full support and co-operation of the exemplary individuals featured in this book.

They neither paid nor received any payment for their co-operation, but chose to give freely of their valuable time and share their sound wisdom on ways to achieve success. My thanks to all of these leaders in their respective fields.

I'm also especially grateful to the many people, who decided to support this project by placing advance purchase orders for Winning Ways, sight unseen. Some participants placed no orders but gave valuable insight regarding achieving success.

The purchase orders we received in advance allowed us to govern our print runs efficiently and cost-effectively, ensuring enough books to meet demand but avoid a large inventory.

My thanks go to DeFeo Auto Service; realtor John DiLiberto; Dr. Tony Mancuso; Ken Lindsay and Mortgage Financial; Sam Mercanti and CARSTAR Automotive; Ray ('Ray on Ray South') Puder and Mortgage Financial; Ramada Plaza Hotel, Sahar's Hospitality Inc., Rudy and Teresa Reimer; Rudy K. Reimer; J. D. (Jim) Rundle, MBA, CGA, Certified General Accountant; and White Hat Inc.

As well, I appreciate the assistance extended by many conscientious people, too numerous to mention, in bringing this book to fruition.

My thanks, as always, to my wife Philippa for her faith and encouragement in my endeavours.
- **Michael B. Davie.**

Cover Photo Credits:

This book featured alternating cover photos.
Cover/interior photo credits are as follows:

WhiteHat Inc.: Courtesy of WhiteHat.
Dr. Tony Mancuso: Photo by Paul Sparrow.
Junior Achievement: Courtesy Junior Achievement.
Rudy Reimer and Family: Paul Sparrow.
Ken Lindsay/Mortgage Financial: Michael B. Davie.
CARSTAR/Sam Mercanti: Courtesy CARSTAR.
John DiLiberto: Courtesy Adele DiLiberto

Winning Ways

Vol. 2: More of The Right Stuff

Success In South Central Ontario

Michael B. Davie

Manor House Publishing Inc.

Great books by Michael B. Davie:

All titles published by Manor House Publishing Inc., unless
indicated otherwise.

Non-fiction

News & Features Vol. 1
Award-winning Journalism

Winning Ways Vol. 2
More of the Right Stuff

Winning Ways Vol. 1
The Right Stuff

Bushwhacked
Coping with the American Superpower
And other Post-Cold War Dilemmas

Following The Great Spirit
Exploring Native Indian Belief Systems

Political Losers
In Canada, U.S., Ukraine

Distant Voices
Canadian Politics On the Outside Looking In

Canada Decentralized
Can Our Nation Survive?

Quebec and Section 33
Why The Notwithstanding Clause Must Not Stand

Inside the Witches' Coven
Exploring Wiccan Rituals

Enterprise 2000
Hamilton, Halton, Niagara Embrace the Millennium

Success Stories BR
Business Achievement in Greater Hamilton

Hamilton: It's Happening* BR
Celebrating Hamilton's Sesquicentennial

Fiction/Poetry

Poetry For The Insane

You're on my hit list for calling me
Creep
A Novel

The Late Man
A Novel

Archival

Print History
(Self-published, with more than 60 volumes and over 10,000 pieces of published writings)

BR = Published by BRaSH Publishing
* = With co-author Sherry Sleightholm
# = Written under the pen name I. Murderman

Manor House Publishing Inc.
(905) 648-2193.

Dedicated to:

Achievers everywhere,
Junior and otherwise

About the author

Easily one of Canada's most versatile and prolific writers, Michael B. Davie is the author of such critically acclaimed business books as Enterprise 2000 and Success Stories.

The multi-award-winning writer is also the author of such nationally important books as Canada Decentralized; and Quebec & Section 33: Why the Notwithstanding Clause Must Not Stand.

Other critically acclaimed books include: Distant Voices; Political Losers; Bushwhacked; Inside The Witches' Coven; Following The Great Spirit; and The Late Man, a novel.

Michael B. Davie is also a journalist with The Toronto Star, Canada's largest newspaper, reaching millions of readers daily.

The author has won dozens of awards for outstanding journalism. His work has also appeared in such major Canadian newspapers as the Halifax Chronicle-Herald, Montreal Gazette, Calgary Herald, Winnipeg Free Press, Edmonton Journal and Vancouver Sun.

Prior to The Star, he was an editor with The Globe and Mail, Canada's national newspaper with coast-to-coast readership.

Previous to The Globe, he spent 17 years with The Hamilton Spectator, where he won 28 journalism awards.

Prior to joining The Spectator, he spent five years with other publications, including the daily Welland Tribune where he was a reporter, columnist and editor.

He also served two years as regional news editor for one of Ontario's largest chains of community newspapers.

Born in Hamilton in 1954, Michael B. Davie's interest in writing began in early childhood. As a pre-school child, he became withdrawn and was in a state of shock after his parents decided to divorce. His withdrawn behaviour became cause for concern and he was placed under observation by psychologists. At one point, the child opened the door to a room to find child psychologists had been studying him through two-way mirrors.

Davie then began closely observing other children and adults, studying their interaction and watching their stories unfold. By the late 1960s and into the 1970s, while in his teens, he was already a contributing writer to counter culture publications.

He turned professional in the mid-1970s as Editor of The Phoenix serving Mohawk College of Applied Arts & Technology where he earned a Broadcast Journalism diploma.

He also holds a Niagara College Print Journalism diploma and degrees in Political Science from McMaster University where he was repeatedly named to the Deans' Honour List and won the Political Science Prize for outstanding academic achievement.

Michael B. Davie currently resides in Ancaster with his wife Philippa and their children Donovan, Sarah and Ryan.

Contents

Manor House Publishing Inc.
(905) 648-2193

Introduction

The right stuff. Successful people quite obviously have it. But what is it? Where is it? And how do you get it?

Much like the first highly popular, critically acclaimed Winning Ways volume, this new volume – Winning Ways Vol. 2: More Of The Right Stuff – looks at the stories behind the success stories.

Once again we examine how they overcame great odds to become leaders in their respective fields.

As you make your way through this much-awaited second volume, you'll encounter a generous amount of information about earning wealth, about achieving lasting success, about making dreams come true and conquering any obstacles in the way.

None of the participants telling their stories paid to go into this book. Nor did we pay them for their valuable advice and insight.

Instead, we selected some leading businesses, organizations, entrepreneurs and professionals – all leaders in their respective fields – to contribute to a discussion on the qualities that add up to success.

Some significant developments have taken place since the last book, including the amalgamation of Junior Achievement organizations in Halton and Niagara to form Junior Achievement of South Central Ontario – JASCO for short.

I set out writing this book in an effort to benefit JASCO by creating a book filled with useful advice and tips youth can draw on for inspiration and education while setting on the road to success. This book also opens with a chapter on JA in hopes this worthy organization can make use of donated copies to promote its programs.

But somewhere along the way – the winning way – I again found I too was learning a great deal about how to treat people and how to achieve success. This book is also of benefit to the population at large. It's a great chance to learn from those who have achieved lasting success in their respective fields.

Simply put, this book is for all of us.

After reading in detail about the life stories, trials and tribulations encountered by our chapter participants, you'll find each chapter ends with a series of their tips for success. It's truly valuable reading that is sure to inspire and educate everyone.

The featured success stories in this book include: Rosaleen Citron and partners at WhiteHat Inc., a leading information technology security provider; Sam Mercanti and the highly successful CARSTAR Automotive Canada; booming mortgage broker Ken Lindsay and Mortgage Financial; dentist Dr. Tony Mancuso; prominent real estate agent John DiLiberto; and leading commercial developer Rudy Reimer plus his entrepreneurial wife and son, who have each achieved their own enviable measures of success and have some interesting and insightful tips of their own to share.

The successful people filling the chapters of this book know the importance of JA: Sharing one's insight with youth helps ensure the arrival of a new generation of knowledgeable entrepreneurs. Read on.

- **Michael B. Davie.**

Winning Ways 2

Chapter/Profiles
of Successful People

Tips on Achieving Success

A Learning Experience…
for Everyone

Junior Achievement
Of South Central Ontario

Chapter 1

Junior Achievement

Learning to achieve success

"We measure our success in the number of students we can reach by trained volunteers delivering high quality programs."

Bob English, President and CEO,
Junior Achievement of South Central Ontario

At a glance:
Junior Achievement of South Central Ontario:

Founded: In 2003 following the amalgamation of JA charters in Halton and Niagara, which boasted many decades of operation.

Claim to fame: The amalgamation will streamline operations and improve efficiencies in the development and delivery of youth programs. The expanded catchment area now encompasses approximately 234,000 students eligible to participate in various programs that bring business people and youth together to learn the ways of commerce.

Programs: Programs include Business Basics designed for grades 5 and 6, Dollars with Sense for grade 7, Economics of Staying in School for grade 8, and Company Program: A Student Venture geared to secondary students. The secondary program is designed to be delivered both in class, and after school.

Mission: To educate and inspire the youth of South Central Ontario to value free enterprise, to understand business and economic development and to develop entrepreneurial and leadership skills.

For More information:
Contact: Junior Achievement of South Central Ontario HQ: 560 Guelph Line, Burlington, Ont. L7R 3M4.
Phone: 905-637-7200
Fax: 905-637-5823
Email: info@jascont.org

Chapter 1

Junior Achievement
Learning to achieve success

Bigger and better than ever, the new Junior Achievement of South Central Ontario holds a wealth of opportunities for enterprising youth.

Junior Achievement of South Central Ontario – JASCO for short – is the result of the July 1, 2003 amalgamation of JA charters in Halton and Niagara.

"The new whole is definitely greater than the sum of its parts," asserts Bob English, president and CEO of JASCO.

"We've reduced our costs significantly, improved efficiencies and streamlined our operations," adds English, noting that JASCO is now responsible for the operation & delivery of JA programs in Hamilton, Halton & Niagara.

Sue Suess, JASCO Senior Vice-President, nods in agreement: "We now serve an area stretching from Fort Erie to Oakville," Suess notes. "With approximately 234,000 students in our expanded catchment area, we have plenty of room to grow and we're now one of the largest regional charters in Canada."

JASCO has its headquarters in Burlington, in the offices of the former JA Halton. There is also a branch office in St. Catharines and JA programs are made available in schools throughout Hamilton, Halton and Niagara.

Goal To Reach 10,800 Students

English, notes the three former JA entities combined approximately 6,000 student-participants. "The goal now is to reach over 10,800 in the post-amalgamation Junior Achievement. We have strong support from all communities and are confident that sponsorship and volunteers will be found to meet our goal.

JASCO is part of a trend to amalgamate JA charters. There were previously 14 JA charters in Ontario. Now there are four, each drawing on the greater resources of their expanded organization.

Across Canada, 32 JA groups have been amalgamated into just 14.

English says the youth programs at JA have also been improved and consolidated, resulting in five superb programs. All five programs are new or have had their format and content refreshed to adhere to a nation-wide JA program needs assessment. Audit systems are also in place to measure the quality and impact of the programs and ensure they're the best they can possibly be.

"We're also concentrating on marketing and outreach to draw more participants and volunteers," notes English, a former senior manager with Bell Canada whose business experience also includes the patenting and marketing of a steel roofing shingle system. He also served as Executive Director of the Canadian Diabetes Association – Central Region.

"Right now, we do not have enough dollars and volunteers to meet the demand for programs," adds English, whose involvement with Junior Achievement dates back to the mid-1970s when he was president of the Mississauga Jaycees and provided volunteer advisors for the Company Program at Junior Achievement of Peel.

"My message to businesses is to please consider supporting Junior Achievement. It's a wonderful organization and it's preparing future generations to meet the challenges of the business world."

Preparing Youth For The Future

Founded in 1919 in Springfield, Mass., Junior Achievement is an international non-profit organization dedicated to educating and inspiring young people about business and economics.

The JA experience gives young people a chance to taste success while helping them discover leadership, entrepreneurial and workforce readiness skills so they can achieve their highest potential. The aim is to prepare youth to enjoy future successes as citizens in the global community. JA enjoys the participation of about 4-million children globally.

JA began in Canada in 1955 and became a national organization with the establishment of Junior Achievement of Canada (JACAN) in 1967.

JACAN develops, markets and licenses the JA brand of youth business and economic education programs in Canada through 14-chartered offices. JA programs now reach more than 1.2- million young Canadians in over 400 communities.

JA programs teach youth about business and economics through age appropriate activities that complement class curricula. JA's current program line-up includes programs at the elementary, middle and high school levels.

Junior Achievement is dedicated to partnering the business and education communities. JA offers cost free, curriculum-enhancing programs delivered by trained and inspiring volunteers who share their practical experience to equip students with the necessary skills to enter tomorrow's workforce and to face their futures with confidence.

Junior Achievement is funded by corporate sponsors who believe in the mission and vision of JA. Junior Achievement also receives government grants to advance the delivery of programs as well as relying on contributions from individual donors.

Annually more than 11,000 Canadians volunteer with JA, helping young people understand how business and economics really work.

English says business leaders who still question whether they can afford the time or money to support JA aren't asking the right question.

Volunteer Involvement Crucial

"The real question is can you afford not to be involved," English asserts. "Today's students are tomorrow's leaders, tomorrows employers, and tomorrows workforce. We know that today's young people

will replace us in business, government and all profes-
sions. We need to make sure these young people are
ready to face the many challenges ahead of them."

Junior Achievement volunteers are the key to
the success of the organization. JA volunteers come
from all areas of business and bring with them commitment, experience, perspective and enthusiasm.

All JA Volunteers receive professional training
and use tested program materials to help facilitate a JA
program in a classroom or help a group of teenagers
operate a business. Volunteers often enhance their own
communication; facilitation and leadership skills, while
helping the future leaders of tomorrow gain new skills.

With the exception of JA's Company Program-
A Student Venture after school edition, all of the
programs are delivered during school hours and as
such, volunteers are committed to delivering the program during the workday.

To become a JA Volunteer, call the JA office:
905-637-7200. Email: volunteers@jascont.org.

JA Programs Develop Young Minds

English notes JA programs help to shape young
minds and assist students in developing the ability to
recognize opportunity, take initiative, tolerate risk, and
to think and act independently.

Suess says it's important for young people to
understand what it takes to run a business; because it's
likely they'll need entrepreneurial skills when the time
comes to making a living.

"Students today face the challenge of preparing for
a rapidly changing economy – they need an early start

to be ready to meet society's demands," says Suess, noting that JA's carefully designed programs help youth learn about every aspect of business by doing.

She notes that they learn about leadership, marketing, customer service, budgeting, managing money, developing entrepreneurial skills and the importance of staying in school.

Focus on all students

English says JASCO is continuing the community desire to have JA programs delivered to students up to grade 12. These are the years when young people face many choices and are expected to make many decisions. Grades 5/6 are years when students are like blotters absorbing new learning's. The world begins to open up, as they better understand the community and what is needed to succeed. As they proceed through grades 7 and 8, life choices begin to emerge. The importance of education is much better understood. In addition, the economics of lifestyle becomes quite clear. In secondary school, young people experience a pivotal time in their lives.

They find positive Junior Achievement programs that give them hands-on experience towards founding and running their own temporary small business venture readily provide direction.

For many of these young people, this is often their first exposure to the business world.

Depending on their background and personal tastes, they may not have ever considered a business career as a meaningful option.

But through JA, they participate in running a business, get their commercial feet wet, gain an understanding of the world of commerce, and are better able to determine if they'd like to consider a career in business as one of their top employment choices.

Helping to create Financial Literacy

JA programs give young people a head start on financial literacy.

English notes the participants receive insight into how to develop good personal finance skills, as well as an appreciation for the workings of business.

"JA gives you the tools you need to help make the decisions to shape your future. The programs are based on real life and they're delivered by business volunteers – the front-line people who make decisions."

Simply put, JA programs are innovative, interactive and fun.

All JA programs meet many of the curriculum outcomes required by educators. JA is one of only a few organizations listed in the Ontario Government document Choices Into Action as being suitable to provide teachers with additional tools for teaching.

Junior Achievement has a strong and successful relationship with the public, private and catholic school boards in Niagara, Hamilton and Halton. At the beginning of each school year, schools are sent information packages and registration forms for JA programs. It is up to the teacher to determine whether or not a JA program will be delivered in his/her classroom.

Exciting Youth Programs

Programs include a Business Basics program offering students in grades 5 and 6 an introduction to the organization and operation of a business.

Guided by a volunteer business consultant, students learn via interactive, fun and age-appropriate activities about the four basic facets of business.

There's also the Dollars With Sense program aimed at students in Grade 7.

This is a new program that equips Grade 7 students with the financial literacy skills necessary to make informed decisions about their futures.

In this program, students reflect on their lives and goals while learning about money management, simple investment strategies and how to make informed decisions. Led by experienced business volunteers, students learn how making responsible choices today will better prepare them for tomorrow.

For students in grades 7 and 8, there's the Economics of Staying In School program encouraging students to look toward the future. This program is specifically designed to help students develop positive attitudes toward education while recognizing the personal and economic costs of living independently.

Volunteers for Junior Achievement in school programs are fully trained in a 1 1/2 hour training session. It takes as little as 1 hour a week for 4 weeks to deliver a basic program. The best part about volunteering is knowing you're making a difference in the lives of youth. Volunteers are expected to take the time (after training) to read through the materials and prepare for the in-class program delivery.

High School Level Company Program

High School programs include the exciting Company Program-A Student Venture. This after-school program is for grades 9-12 and it empowers high school students to experience the risks and rewards of entrepreneurship by creating and operating their own companies.

In fact, the best-known JA program is its flagship Company Program, in which 20 or more high school students get together one evening per week for 22 weeks to found, own and operate their own company.

Students come up with the idea for a company and sell shares to finance their business.

The students then manufacture, market and sell a product.

After the 22 weeks they liquidate the company and the investors are paid back. It's truly experiential learning, based on the premise that the best way to learn anything is to actually do it.

Beyond offering a significant degree of on-the-job experience, the Company Program – under the expert guidance of expert business volunteers – also builds teamwork skills, self-confidence and self-esteem as the company partners work together to choose and market a product; track expenditures and finances; pay bills and wages; and, ideally, go on to achieve the goal of earning a profit.

Through a fast paced experiential learning process that is facilitated by committed volunteers from the business community, students complete a full business cycle.

They learn that to run a successful business they must establish goals and objectives; incorporate and capitalize; organize a Board of Directors and elect Officers; manufacture and market a product or service; maintain a financial record system; pay wages and salaries, commissions and taxes; close books and handle dividend declarations or payments; and, finally, liquidate all assets, settle accounts and prepare a report to their shareholders.

There's also the Company Program, A Student Venture - In Class Edition for grades 10-12. Identical in content, it takes place in the classroom.

Volunteering For The Company Program

Each year many adult volunteers from various businesses and service organizations throughout South Central Ontario work side by side with teenagers from grades 9 to 12.

As a team of four to six volunteer advisors, you'll help a company of 20 to 25 teenagers start up and operate a real business, providing advice in the areas of company management, production, finance, sales, and human relations.

The Advisor team begins by preparing potential prototype product ideas in the weeks prior to program start-up in October.

By researching potential costs, you're able to help the Achievers as they prepare to make important decisions in launching their new company.

In the first 3 weeks of program, the Achievers will have elected their company's management team, chosen a start-up product and completed a detailed business plan. By Week 4, they'll have assumed responsibility for all company operations.

Throughout the program, advisors are there as a team each night to help the Achievers as they manage production, sales, audits, and company and Board Meetings.

Liquidation procedures are concluded with the completion of Shareholders' Reports in late April.

Advisor's Time Commitment:

Through September and October, the advisor can expect to be actively involved in team time dedicated to researching potential product ideas.

In late September, there are several advisor team-training sessions in various locations throughout the charter territory.

From mid-October to the end of April there are more than 20 companies meeting on Tuesday and Wednesday nights.

In November there's an officer training session.

And there are other JA events, including the JA Future Unlimited Banquet in late April or early May and the annual meeting advisors won't want to miss.

Total volunteer time: An average of 100 very satisfying and rewarding hours helping today's youth gain business experience.

For the participants, the Company Program opens their eyes to a world of business opportunities and an educational process that for some is a whole lot more interesting and fun than school.

And, speaking of school, another reason the JA program focuses on high school students is to instil a greater appreciation of formal education and help stem dropout rates that in Hamilton alone tend to hover around 30 per cent of the student population

Volunteering is Satisfying

Volunteering to deliver a JA program is one of

the most rewarding experiences possible. Not only do you get to share your time and talent with students, you have an opportunity to develop personal delivery skills. Many volunteers return annually siting the wonderful personal fulfillment that they receive. Suess says that the return rate is well above 75% and the positive feedback from teachers and students provides an additional reward for the volunteers.

Volunteers for the after school program find the experience gratifying because it's their skills and expertise that will help the company reach success.

And it's fun – especially when an advisor team guides a well-organized program that allows every Achiever and advisor to be productively involved in the company. Savvy marketers know the impact of affinity marketing, and JA provides an excellent opportunity to just that with future customers and employers.

Please note that police screening of volunteers is required. Contact JASCO with questions.

In addition to providing the means to deliver a program, sponsorship introduces a company's name and image to a new audience.

Do you have employees that you are planning on sending to a presentation or sales course?

Ask them to volunteer to deliver your JA program instead.

For just a fraction of the cost of those courses, your employees will not only gain good presentation and time management skills, but they will gain a better perspective of your overall company operations by witnessing the learning that goes on.

They'll also likely strengthen their conflict resolution and facilitation skills.

In fact, Junior Achievement itself is by far the oldest and fastest-growing economic education program for young people in the entire world due, in part, to the contribution made by the many caring companies and business people who support this organization that does everything from help kids get a head start in life to assisting them with starting up and running their own small business.

JA True Bargain

Even while increasing its growth rate of active participants, JASCO has also endeavoured to hold the participation costs of its programs, in essence building tomorrow's business leaders at yesterday's prices.

All JA programs emphasize the importance of a good education. The JA programs also help students develop positive attitudes and enthusiasm for the necessity of lifelong learning.

And all of the participants' temporary companies fulfill the JA mandate of providing their youthful business executives with the rewarding experience of operating a company; producing, marketing and selling products; and managing inventory, costs, revenue and consumer demand.

The true-to-life business experience has a way of bringing out hidden talents in student participants while helping them to believe in themselves.

Volunteers, Sponsors Wanted

Volunteers and sponsors are appreciated. And more are needed to make programs a reality for as many students as JASCO can reach out to.

By donating their time and resources, their expert advice and willingness to help, these volunteer business people provide the essential guidance needed to steer participants' businesses on the road to success. Some of the business volunteers also pay sponsorship fees to fund programs.

The cost of sponsorship really isn't all that expensive. Not when you consider a company can divert just a fraction of the funds it would normally devote to sending personnel to conferences instead of supporting JA.

Perhaps the biggest difference between putting money into a conference and sponsoring JA is that the money spent on JA is an investment in youth that is sure to have lasting value.

And the benefits aren't all one-sided: In providing a staff member – or yourself – as a JA volunteer business expert, you're taking part in an exercise that will confer leadership growth and organizational benefits to your own company.

Why do the volunteers donate so much of themselves: They understand the importance of JA.

Simply put, an investment in JA today is an investment in the business leaders of tomorrow.

Top 10 reasons for being a JA Volunteer:

10. Receive instant feedback on your communication skills.

9. Network with members of the business community and education communities.

8. Receive professional training to ensure your success in delivering a program.

7. Possibly the only meeting on your schedule, where everyone is excited to see you.

6. Influence the young people who will become the future workforce.

5. Share your experiences, mistakes and successes with future leaders.

4. Help build tomorrow's business leaders by serving as a mentor.

3. Enhance your personal communication & facilitation skills.

2. Contribute something real and of value to your community.

1. The kids need you!

Leanne Bucaro, Thomas Slodichak, Rosaleen Citron
and Alan McLaren of WhiteHat Inc.

Chapter 2

WhiteHat

The Cyber Space Good Guys

"WhiteHat is an ITSP, an Information Technology Security Provider, and our mandate is to arm our clients to go into cyber battle."

- Rosaleen Citron.

At a Glance:
Rosaleen Citron and WhiteHat:

Rosaleen Citron
Age: 47
Title: CEO and founder of WhiteHat Inc., an industry-leading information technology security provider.
Claim to fame: Ranking two consecutive years among the top 100 women business owners by Profit and Chatelaine magazines and nominated by Ernst and Young for Entrepreneur of the Year for 2003, Citron heads a major, fast-growing IT security company. Products and services are aimed at a wide array of security-conscious clients, including Fortune 500 firms, governments and law enforcement agencies across North America.
Financial Data: Largely undisclosed. However, this is a successful private company with major clients that does millions of dollars in business annually.
Partners: Alan McLaren , president; Leanne Bucaro, executive vice-president, operations/ communications; and, Tom Slodichak, chief security officer.
For More information:
Contact: WhiteHat Inc: 1-800-561-3270
Fax: 1-888-828-9588
Address: 1100 Burloak Drive, Penthouse, Burlington, Ontario, Canada, L7L 6B2.
Website: www.whitehatinc.com
Email: security@whitehatinc.com
For customer support:
1-800-561-3270.
Fax: 1-905-332-6673
Email: security@whitehatinc.com

Chapter 2

WhiteHat

The Cyberspace Good Guys

Cyberspace good guys WhiteHat Inc. come to the rescue when black hats – hackers – try to breech online security.

In the very security-conscious, post 9-11 world, Burlington-based WhiteHat Inc. is an industry-leading IT – information technology– security provider.

In an age of hackers and viruses and identity thieves, WhiteHat's CEO and founder, Rosaleen Citron, knows her firm plays a vital role in protecting clients and the general public.

"WhiteHat is an ITSP, an Information Technology Security Provider, and our mandate is to arm our clients to go into cyber battle," asserts Citron, who has placed among Profit and Chatelaine magazines' Top 100 Women Business Owners for 2002 and 2003.

"The global worry is cyber-terrorism – the fear that someone will hack their way into an IT system and take down a hydro power grid or hit a nuclear power plant and cause a melt-down or cause some other damage that would throw everything into chaos," she states, noting her company provides layered security systems to detect and thwart hackers.

"Our daily battles are staying one step ahead of the black hat hackers.," she adds.

"In the WhiteHat world things move as fast as the Internet and it never stops," Citron asserts in an interview at WhiteHat's 10,000-square-foot penthouse offices in one of the original Reimer towers at the Burlington-Oakville border off the Queen Elizabeth Way highway.

The impressive offices also boast a panoramic view of Lake Ontario, Hamilton, Niagara and Toronto regions.

Citron Provides Vision

As CEO, Citron oversees the overall vision of the company and is heavily involved in the corporation's day-to-day activities.

Her insight and clarity have been featured in the Globe & Mail, Toronto Star, the Business Journal, The Wall Street Reporter and numerous trade publications, along with television media CP24, CTV, CBC and CNN.

She's also a sought-after speaker on IT security and other business matters at speaking engagements across North America.

"One of the main things I do is help our partners and the public understand the need for security in today's high-tech marketplace," notes Citron, an active member of the Computer Security Institute (CSI) and the Information System Security Association (ISSA).

And the need for IT security is great: Imagine hackers deleting corporate files, wiping out health records, damaging military data, shutting down many airports or power grids, accessing your bank accounts or credit cards or stealing your identity. The potential damage and ramifications are enormous.

WhiteHat Offers Many Products, Services

To protect its clients, WhiteHat offers best-of-breed and market-leader security products, such as: audit and assessment; authorization; content filtering; enterprise security; and virus protection software and products; plus numerous firewalls, forensic tools, host-based intrusion detection products, Internet security products, wireless security and forensic tools.

WhiteHat also provides a range of services, including product installations, administration and configuration services.

Professional services are also offered, including security education programs.

As well, WhiteHat CISSP certified security professionals provide security policy and secure network architecture services along with incident response and attack-penetration services. WhiteHat has been granted Enhanced Reliability Security Status by the federal government.

Security services capabilities include enterprise security assessments – host vulnerability, wireless security and attack and penetration assessments – along with consulting services and can even include sending in a WhiteHat Computer Incident Response Team (CIRT) and computer forensic analysis and investigation. WhiteHat also provides professional security training and is a training centre for many best-of-breed security product manufacturers.

Various service packages are available, including WhiteHat's White Glove Service, which allows clients to reduce the number of security vendors they deal with, consolidate maintenance contracts, receive recommendations regarding tested potential product replacements and get access to up-to-date technology.

WhiteHat even co-ordinates contract billings and terminations, allowing the client to focus on their core business with one less administrative headache.

For a growing number of corporations, dealing with WhiteHat means dealing with a one-stop, single-source for all their IT security needs.

An Entrepreneurial Upbringing

How Citron came to head the leading IT security provider is a story that begins in England.

Citron was born in 1955 in London to Jeffrey and Elizabeth Citron, active and industrious entrepreneurs.

"I learned a lot from my parents at an early age," Citron smiles. "They both had an incredible work ethic and 12-hour days meant nothing to them. I think I also got my entrepreneurial bent and sense of independence from them as they were risk-taking business people."

One fateful risk her parents took was immigrating to Canada and Burlington in 1965.

In 1976, at age 21, Citron decided to start her own business, Citron Real Estate. She spent the next seven years running her company, which marketed and sold newly constructed homes. Then, in 1983, at the tender age of 28, she retired from the business.

Short-lived Retirement

"I thought I'd retire and have enough money to last the rest of my life – it lasted six months and I ran out of money," Citron chuckles. "I did a little too much expensive travelling, and to be honest, I was bored silly and really needed to get back into business."

In 1984, Citron's parents introduced her to a representative from Computer Associates – now a multi-billion-dollar company – who recognized her potential on the sales front and enrolled her in the firm's training camp. A full time job at CA followed.

"I've long had a passion and fascination for high technology," Citron explains. "We live in a world of endless change and opportunity. Every time I've had an opportunity, I've seized it."

In 1989, after five years with CA, Citron joined a newly founded Bell Canada subsidiary, IIS (Intelligent Information Systems) Technologies, which found goods and services for Bell and the Bell family of companies and also marketed Bell's own internally developed systems to outside markets.

But in 1993, Bell Canada went through a corporate restructuring and decided to concentrate on its core telecommunications business.

Citron Founds 4COMM

When Citron learned IIS was going to be closed, she offered to take over the division and operate it as an independent company, with Bell as a major customer. This marked the founding of 4COMM Inc.

"I set my goals when I was in my early 30's. Some of the things I put down sounded out of reach at the time, but I exceeded them," says Citron. "One of my goals was to run my own technology company. That was in my five year plan."

"Within two years," Citron continues, "I was sitting at my desk at Bell Canada when opportunity came knocking, and if I can give anyone a piece of advice, when opportunity comes knocking don't walk to open the door. Run to the door and open it wide."

Citron was confident of her success.

"I truly believed that we could make a go of the business and on April 3 1993, we launched 4COMM, the progenitor of WhiteHat and I was running my first high tech company. And we managed even in a challenging economy to grow."

The former division had devoted about 90 per cent of its attention to communications technology and about 10 per cent to Information Technology security.

But with 4COMM, the equation was reversed and security became 90 per cent of the focus. "We just saw how big this was going," Citron explains, noting how quickly her firm emerged as a leader in an industry still in its infancy, developing its own website in 1994, three years before AOL even existed. Indeed, Citron was truly instrumental in pioneering enterprise-wide security solutions for Fortune 500 companies.

Former DigiDyne IT company partner Tom Slodichak, who loves the security aspect of IT, joined 4COMM in 1997 and the firm became even more focused on IT security. But as Citron notes, it wasn't all smooth sailing. "After a few years we moved heavily into the IT security niche and we discovered that distributed computing brought with it a lot of issues."

IT Security Challenges

Citron notes that within a few years, the firm had become exclusively devoted to IT security. "We got really good at this," she smiles, "and we wanted to change the look and feel of our company, how do you do this?, well you can get funding and go out and create a new model, or you could merge or be acquired. We took the path of least resistance which was being acquired during the .com boom which went dot gone. What a disaster."

"Most people might have watched the company and millions of dollars go down the drain and just give up," she adds, shaking her head. "Not me, I have goals that I must reach. So, taking what money I had left I poured it into founding my new company."

WhiteHat Inc. Is Born

A new name and corporate image reflecting the security role were badly needed. In May of 2001, Citron founded WhiteHat Inc. The WhiteHat name is inspired by cowboys of silver screen. The good guys always wore a white hat, the bad guys wore black hats. That descriptive terminology has now been applied to the IT world.

"I opened WhiteHat right after the dot-gone period in 2001, the market was tanking, businesses stopped spending and jobs disappeared," She recalls. "Then we had the three horseman of the apocalypse: We've had 9-11, the Iraq War, and SARS."

"Life keeps throwing challenges at us," Citron notes. "SARS has been particularly painful to our bottom line. None of our US students would come for training and in the first month of the outbreak we lost close to $100,000 of our security education revenue."

"However," she adds, "on the flip side we had

trade shows and conferences we were working with our US partners, who were concerned and opted out of staffing their expensive booths. So, in one show we ended up running their booths for them and because of this we got all of the leads."

Happily, both the WhiteHat name and the IT security company itself have proven successful.

As Citron recalls: "Out of each disaster in our lives we learn something and sometimes fate takes a hand. During the acquisition of my company I had an opportunity to meet some very talented people. Once I was up and running I had the opportunity to go back and convince those people to join me in my WhiteHat adventure. Today they are my business partners. And I am incredibly proud of them and our business. We have just entered our third year and even in this economy our second year grew by 100 per cent not just in revenue but staff as well not a small feat. And, we were actually profitable."

Slodichak Invaluable Component

Citron says Slodichak was and is an invaluable component to WhiteHat's ongoing success.

As chief security officer of WhiteHat Inc., Slodichak oversees and directs: professional services teams; security education and product and partner support programs, before and after sales.

He also monitors and researches trends in the security industry and quickly adapts to this ever evolving market to ensure the highest quality of security service for the company's partners.

Slodichak has several decades of perspective on the evolution of computer technologies and security issues and earns the trust of clients by delivering security solutions that work in real-world applications. He began his career at McGill University as a teaching assistant in artificial intelligence and as a freelance computer programmer.

He furthered his technical knowledge as a research assistant by developing microprocessor-based data reduction and analysis systems. After graduating from McGill with a B.Sc First Class Honours, he continued building his expertise and in 1980 became a founding partner of DigiDyne Inc. He joined 4comm Inc. in 1997 as a partner, helping establish it as a premier vendor of data security products and services.

Slodichak is also a CISSP (Certified Information Systems Security Professional), an active member of the CSI (Computer Security Institute) and ISSA (Information Systems Security Association). He's also completed certification requirements as a SCSP (Symantec Certified Security Professional) and he's an established authority who helps guide the public and corporations in security related issues. He's appeared as an IT security expert in numerous technology trade publications and is a frequent contributor to Industry magazine. He's also appeared on electronic media, including CP24 and CTV Newsnet.

With Slodichak on board, Citron then turned her attention to bringing in additional partners with additional skill sets.

Leanne Bucaro, Media Expert

One of the additional partners that Citron was eager to acquire was Leanne Bucaro. The two had met years earlier while Citron was doing business for

4COMM and they developed a mutual liking and respect for each other's abilities and personalities.

A seasoned public relations professional, Bucaro began her career writing for the film and television industry, moved into advertising and then moved once again into corporate communications with the Ontario provincial government.

Having excelled in various management positions, Bucaro next moved into the high-tech market with Bell Mobility where she was instrumental in the launch of Digital PCS. She was also with the senior management team responsible for launching Bell World, the retail distribution company for Bell Mobility, Bell Canada and Bell Express Vu.

She's also an active member of the International Association of Business Communicators (IABC), the Women's Executive Network and CWC (Canadian Women in Communications). And, she's been nominated for the Top 40 Under 40 business award.

Bucaro, a slender, attractive blonde, was a well-spoken, intelligent communicator and media magnet. She had been working at an IT company as Director of public relations and investor relations and, in early September 2001, was enjoying a rare vacation, a four-week stay in Europe that began in mid-August.

Fate Smiles On Bucaro

While relaxing poolside at an Italian villa, Bucaro took a phone call and discovered the IT company she worked for was going under and she wouldn't be paid salary and vacation pay owed to her. But they still hoped she'd attend a meeting at the NASDAQ stock exchange offices at the World Trade Centre in New York. The meeting was set for September 11.

"Since the company wasn't going to pay me the salary they owed me or pay for the trip, I told them there was no way I was going," Bucaro says in an interview at WhiteHat headquarters.

"So, by the grace of God, I wasn't at the World Trade Centre on September 11, 2001 – but we lost a lot of friends that day," she adds with a shudder. "I was just walking around in shock, crying. It stunned me into silence."

Bucaro says Citron called her home, fearing she may have been at the WTC when the planes hit the twin towers. "As we were talking, and grieving our missing friends, she reminded me she wanted me to work with her and I took the job."

Bucaro Named Executive Vice-President

The job?: Executive vice-president and partner. Bucaro oversees the development and implementation of all external corporate communications. She is responsible for all media, corporate and public education programs; business development, operations; and marketing. And communicating with the media.

For example, when the 'I Love You' virus hit computer systems, Bucaro rose at 5 am at the horse farm she resides at with husband Mario in rural Milton. She quickly sent out advisory press releases addresses the issue, then spent the rest of the day setting up and being interviewed by CBC The National; CTV; CITY TV, numerous radio stations, plus the Toronto Star, Toronto Sun, National Post and The Globe & Mail.

She's also made frequent appearances on CP24 and CTV NewsNet and CNN plus numerous industry trade publications.

WhiteHat is today a recognized expert in the field of IT security and security issues.

"WhiteHat receives a tremendous amount of 'industry expert' media in TV, Radio and Print – in fact we have been in the trade related publications on a regular basis for well over a year," notes Citron whose company has experienced steady growth since its 2001 founding. By 2003, it employed 20 people at its head office in Burlington, plus an additional 45 consultants operating across North America.

"For security reasons, we can't divulge much information at all about our clients," Bucaro notes. "The challenge was getting the WhiteHat name out there without talking about our clients."

Citron says Bucaro was more than up for that challenge. "With all of the publicity and air time and newspaper space that Leanne attracts, she's given us a $70-million brand," asserts Citron.

Indeed, as WhiteHat executive vice-president, Bucaro has proven to be the principal catalyst to promote the development of the globally competitive information technology security provider. Simply put, she's helped put WhiteHat on the security map.

WhiteHat The 'Go-To' Experts

With the "dot.com meltdown" in 2001, a lot of IT firms went under and major companies and agencies wondered who they could trust, who would still be in business the next day.

"We established WhiteHat as the go-to experts," Bucaro asserts, noting that the company does not hire ex-hackers as no one working for WhiteHat can have a criminal record. Instead it trains its own people to become experts in the way hackers think and function.

"Our IT people are trained in security and we have three CISSPs (Certified Information Systems Security Professionals) on staff, and they're out in the field with recent experience tracking changes in the hacker world to stay on top of their activities."

Bucaro notes WhiteHat will find clients the best products and services that suit their needs and replace obsolete security products.

Alan McLaren Management Expert

To round out the skills of her executive team Citron sought out an individual she'd known many years socially and in business. "I had always wanted to work with Alan and had followed his successful career over the years," Citron notes. "When the opportunity came up I proposed that Alan join us in this wonderful business we were building."

McLaren was pleased: "I've known Rosaleen for almost 20 years and always respected the success she had in business. When she asked me to assist her with the sales strategies of her new venture I decided that I would be willing to offer my consulting services for a few weeks."

"In these two weeks, " he adds, "I interviewed each employee with the express objective of improving the sales process. A few weeks after I presented my findings to Rosaleen, she asked me to join WhiteHat and implement the strategies I'd recommended. After seeing the talent at WhiteHat Inc. I couldn't pass up the opportunity and decieded to join Rosaleen, Tom and Leanne as a business partner."

WhiteHat president Alan McLaren, joined a few months after Bucaro, in December 2001. McLaren is responsible for sales and vendor relationships as well as guiding and delivering on WhiteHat's vision of supplying mission critical security software and hardware solutions, with professional and educational security services to firms and governments worldwide.

He concentrates on extending and optimizing WhiteHat's core competencies and operating excellence. McLaren, who has an athletic background, draws on his natural abilities to lead by example while fostering a team spirit and environment. With nearly two decades of experience in corporate management, a strong background of sales, operations, marketing and information technology, McLaren is a key member of the WhiteHat executive team.

Prior to joining WhiteHat, McLaren gained experience in various capacities with Canon Canada, Savin Corporation and IKON Office Solutions. His corporate experience includes working and living in Ontario, Quebec and Nova Scotia. He's also travelled extensively throughout North America, giving him a keen appreciation for regional and national issues.

McLaren was also a former president of IKON Quebec which provided great experience as he was responsible for integrating seven acquisitions in to IKON Quebec as part of his mandate. "Dealing with true entrepreneurs in Quebec allowed me to understand the challenges and opportunities inherit with owning your own business," he asserts.

"As a corporate manager I never fully appreciated the true business owner dealing with basic issues like making payroll. Large firms never have the perspective of the entrepreneur. The key is to keep the sprit of the entrepreneur alive while adding the corporate controls needed to effectively grow a business. It's a balance that we are living at WhiteHat."

McLaren has been active in media engagements speaking on topics from Identity Theft to Privacy and Security. He is often quoted in industry publications and has been interviewed on various Security topics with both CP 24 (TV) and CBC International (Radio).

An active member of the Young Presidents Organization Ontario (YPO), and a committed family man, Alan has achieved a wonderful balance in his life between business, community and family.

I love what we're building at WhiteHat; a strong business built on good fundamentals. "It all starts with people," Alan states. "As Jim Collins (author of *Good to Great*) puts it "before you deicide where the bus is going you have to make sure you have the right people on the bus. "I know we are putting the right people on our bus. What a ride!"

Promising Future For WhiteHat

The partners agree the future of WhiteHat looks bright indeed, given heightened awareness of computer viruses and societal vulnerability to terrorism.

Although 9-11 prompted governments and firms everywhere to invest in physical security systems, Bucaro notes many companies and agencies are also investing in IT security, as confidential information can be a powerful weapon in the wrong hands.

"With 9-11, we had a wake-up call that told us we're not in Kansas anymore," Bucaro observes. "It raised everyone's security consciousness. We learned that we can't afford to be lax about security of any kind. We need to be diligent and alert – always watching out for hackers and identity thieves – we can't be caught asleep at the switch."

Bucaro notes there's more public acceptance of security delays at airports, post-9-11. She also notes government legislation setting privacy standards for financial/personal/health records should also increase demand for WhiteHat's services. "The legislation will be a vehicle for growing the company," she suggests.

"People need to understand that we live in an age of convenience when you can order something by credit card on the internet or over the phone like that," she says, snapping her fingers.

"And you can also lose your identity like that," she adds, again snapping her fingers.

"We're reaching out to companies and citizens – and it's a growing business," Bucaro notes.

"We need to get the information out – it's the reason why we have our websites and why we do so many public speaking engagements," she adds

"Think of it this way: Every time you open a computer portal, you open a potential security hole."

Computer Chips Everywhere

Citron notes IT is something of a double-edged sword. It brings many benefits and conveniences, but we can also become overly dependent on it and find ourselves inconvenienced when it breaks down.

"When I was just starting out in IT, home PC's were just coming out, and now the average is 2.2 computers per household in Canada," she notes.

"Actually it's a lot more than that because we don't own an appliance, car, stereo, clock or other goods that doesn't have a computer chip in it. The average household has at least 30 microprocessors," she adds.

"You have to stay ahead of the hackers and be diligent when using the Internet," notes Citron who, along with Bucaro, has also served on the Prime Minister's Task Force On Women Entrepreneurs.

"But that goes for everyone. You need to know how to protect your identity from I.D. thieves. You should also learn how to protect your children and teach them how to web-surf safely."

Free Advisory Website

To help educate the public, WhiteHat has a free advisory website: www.whitehatadvisory.com that dispenses information and advice on controlling email, pc security, Internet safety and travel security along with details on viruses such as Trojans and Worms.

Citron says promoting WhiteHat's services to non-tech executives is just another challenge.

"Part of our job," she explains, "is to take what our IT security community says and translate it to plain English, so I am also known as the universal geek speak translator."

And despite the challenges of battling new generations of viruses in a constantly changing environment, Citron wouldn't have it any other way.

"It's a 24/7 lifestyle – being in IT today is an exciting and growing opportunity that I love," Citron states with enthusiasm.

"In fact it can be classified as pure excitement punctuated by moments of stark raving terror," she adds. "I like being the cyberspace good guys, I love doing what we do."

WhiteHat tips for success:

1. Set your goals and live by them – Follow through in everything. Pick your hero's or role models wisely and try to emulate them.

2. Don't be afraid to make mistakes, knowledge is learning what not to do.

3. Run don't walk when opportunity knocks, whether it is in your career or with your potential life mate. Embrace opportunity.

4. Be a team player even if you are a leader – In this market lone wolves take time and energy and companies don't have the resources. Get really good at what you do and work with others to help them; it will go a long way in the near future.

5. Know something about everything and everything about something.

6. Get as many certifications as you can. These are important to your future employers and can provide a huge boost to your self esteem.

7. Do sweat the details. They're important.

8. Keep your options open: We live in an intimate global economy. Technology brings people together in seconds. Your dream job could be in Canada, the UK, South America, Australia, anywhere. Stay open to relocation as a potentially enriching opportunity.

9. Give something back: Be kind and generous to people. Be nice – you never know what will come of it.

10. Bring your dynamic energy to your business. For those just starting out, do business with a full tilt bogey, hair-on-fire attitude.

11. When you pick you life mate, soul mate, or business partner make sure you're ready to emotionally support each other in your life choices.

12. Constantly further your education. Life-long learning is essential. Most successful people never stop learning. People who stay at the top of their game will always come out ahead.

John and Adele DiLiberto

Chapter 3

John DiLiberto

Bringing Out-Of-Town Buyers Home

"People from Mississauga and Toronto and elsewhere are just astonished at the low prices here and the amount of value they're getting at such small cost... They have a difficult time believing they can really buy a great home for so little."

- John DiLiberto

At a Glance:
John DiLiberto, realtor:

John DiLiberto
Title: Associate Real Estate Broker at Re/Max Escarpment Realty Inc., Realtor; MVA: Market Value Appraiser; and RRS: Registered Relocation Specialist.
Claim to fame: DiLiberto specializes in out-of-town buyers, introducing them to the high-value, low-cost properties that can be found throughout the greater Hamilton-Burlington area. He's also one of the top selling realtors in Canada and has been named to the real estate Hall of Fame. He's also a member of the 100% Club and the Platinum Club, both honouring excellence in real estate sales. DiLiberto is a strong community supporter. His advertising on DARTS (Disabled Regional Transit System) buses provides considerable revenue for this worthy organization, supporting and improving the lives of the handicapped. DiLiberto ranks among the top real estate agents, locally and for all of Canada.
Personal: Resides in Hamilton in a West Mountain neighbourhood with wife Adele. The couple have three children: Julie, 29; Joe, 27; and Nick, 21.
For More information:
Contact: John DiLiberto, Re/Max Escarpment Realty (905) 575-5478. Fax: (905) 575-7217.
Address: 550 Fennell Avenue East, Suite 221A, Hamilton, Ontario, L8V 4S9.
Website: www.johndiliberto.com.
Email: johndiliberto@remaxescarpment.com

Chapter 3

John DiLiberto

Bringing Out-Of-Town Buyers Home

Imagine discovering that you can buy the home of your dreams for a fraction of what you anticipated paying. Suddenly you can buy the home you *really* want – more home at less cost.

John DiLiberto makes that dream come true for hundreds of homebuyers every year.

DiLiberto is a top-selling realtor specializing in introducing out-of-town buyers to the high-value, low-cost real estate that can be found throughout the greater Hamilton-Burlington area. He brings them to their new home – the home of their dreams.

Although he also delights local buyers with well-priced, good-value homes, it's the out-of-towners whose jaws drop when he brings them to the promised land hugging the head of Lake Ontario.

"People from Mississauga and Toronto and elsewhere are just astonished at the low prices here and the amount of value they're getting at such small cost," DiLiberto smiles during a recent interview. "They have a difficult time believing they can really buy a great home for so little."

"It's fun," adds the associate broker at Re/Max Escarpment Realty Inc., his smile widening to a grin. "They get so pumped up when they realize these beautiful homes they're seeing are available at prices that are considerably below what they'd be paying for the same house in their old community. Sometimes the difference is literally half the price."

This is what DiLiberto enjoys most: Delighting homebuyers by finding them the best home for them within their price range.

"I find there's a lot of satisfaction in helping people buy or sell homes," he says, "and I'm truly there to help them make what for most people is the biggest transaction in their lives. It's very emotional and inspiring at the same time – and I really enjoy it."

The Rise To Real Estate Excellence

DiLiberto also makes the real estate sales experience enjoyable to buyers and sellers.

If you own a dog, count on DiLiberto to arrive with doggie treats in hand – along with a wealth of market information and proven strategies to sell your home. His approach is consistently friendly, professional and courteous – and it's helped make him one of the top real estate sales people in the entire country.

How DiLiberto rose to such real estate heights is a story that begins in Racalmuto, a small town of about 8,000 people on the southern tip of the island of Sicily in Italy.

John DiLiberto was born to Joe and Jose DiLiberto in 1950 in this quiet agricultural community, where horses and donkeys were then a more common sight on its narrow streets than cars.

The community is in a scenic region, not far from historic Roman ruins.

"A lot of people came to Hamilton from Racalmuto," DiLiberto adds.

"If you add in the sons and daughters of immigrants who came here, I think there's three times as many people from Racalmuto here in Hamilton now as live in that town today."

In fact, so many thousands have immigrated to Hamilton over the years, that in 1993, Murray Street in downtown Hamilton was officially renamed Corso Racalmuto by Hamilton City Council.

A New Life In Hamilton

In 1955, the DiLiberto family joined the throngs of immigrants heading to Canada and they made their way straight to Hamilton.

"I cannot thank my parents enough for moving here and making possible the opportunities I've encountered," DiLiberto asserts.

"My parents have given me wonderful values

and encouragement and support throughout my life."

The family settled into a home in the North End of Hamilton, on Bay Street North at Simcoe Street. John DiLiberto, then 5, enrolled in the Hamilton Catholic school system from kindergarten on.

As John entered his teens, the family moved to the floor above a variety store his parents purchased on Cannon Street between Wentworth Street and Sanford Avenue.

It was home until he moved out years later (his mother, now a widow, continues to live in the same house although the variety store has long since closed).

After attending Cathedral High School, he switched to Scott Park Secondary for his final years.

During this time, some friends were starting up a band and asked him to be singer.

He bought a microphone and PA system. The Sea Sea Ryders were born.

For the next three years, the five-man cover band – singer, lead guitarist, rhythm guitarist, bassist, keyboards player and drummer – became a regular attraction at local high school and church dances.

"I hadn't done any singing before," DiLiberto recalls with a chuckle.

"But I must have been alright because I was with them for three years. It was fun playing in a band – an unforgettable experience.

John And Adele

One gig was particularly memorable for DiLiberto: The band was performing at Burkholder Church Hall, when an attractive girl in the audience caught the popular 16-year-old singer's eye: It was his future wife Adele.

"We just connected," DiLiberto smiles. "She was there with some girlfriends, we started talking during the intermission. Then we started dating and I knew she was my one and only."

DiLiberto notes Adele would later become his wife, his best friend and would play a crucial, ongoing role in his success in real estate.

While still with the band and dating his future wife, the entrepreneurial bug bit DiLiberto hard.

Opens Waterbeds Business

In the late-1960s, at age 18, he was a restless young man with an urge to go into business, so he and a partner opened Waterbeds Unlimited – the first waterbed store in Hamilton – in the King Street East and Victoria Avenue area of downtown Hamilton.

"I got the idea when I saw waterbeds at the Canadian national Exhibition – they were so new and different – and I thought they'd be easy to sell."

While running his independent waterbeds store – with a staff of employees – DiLiberto was also working as a sales representative for an auto parts supplier on Vine Street. "I've always loved cars," he explains, "and this was a way to get involved in the automotive industry."

In 1971, at age 21, John DiLiberto married his sweetheart and best friend Adele.

The couple would have three children: Julie, 29, a special education teacher; Joe, 27, an up and coming illustrator and graphic novelist who has studied animation; and Nick, 21, now completing his third year of the highly rated animation program at Sheridan College.

Founds Auto Parts Business

Shortly after getting married, DiLiberto closed his waterbeds business to concentrate on the auto parts business, and in 1978, he and a partner opened their own auto parts business: Automotive Parts & Performance on Hester Street on Hamilton Mountain, next to Stan Rowe Furniture.

During the ten years he owned and operated Automotive Parts & Performance, DiLiberto treated his employees to stockcar races and Grey Cup games Ottawa and Montreal.

He also opened a branch store in Stoney Creek. Many of his employees – most say he was the best boss they ever had – would later come to use his services to buy and sell homes.

During this time, he was also beginning to look at the possibility of starting a career in real estate.

"I've always had an infatuation, a fascination with real estate," DiLiberto notes.

"I liked the idea of showing homes and selling them. Your home is your most important asset – not just financially, but emotionally. It's where you live, where you raise your family. It's a big part of your life."

Moving Into Real Estate

In 1988, DiLiberto got out of the automotive business and acted on his fascination for real estate.

He began taking real estate courses at a time when the industry was hiking the number and scope of courses needed to become a licensed real estate agent.

The increased requirements meant additional courses – addressing property management, real estate law, mortgage financing and appraisals – had to be taken over a two-year period and years of experience had to be accumulated.

"At first, I thought that this was my bad luck at the time," DiLiberto recalls, "as here I was having to take these extra courses and get all this added experience when if I'd got in the business just a few months earlier I wouldn't have needed the extra courses."

"Instead, it was a great thing," he adds. "I really enjoyed the courses and I learned a lot. I got 96 per cent in commercial real estate and I ended up taking so many courses that I became a broker in two years and a market value appraiser in five."

He also became an RRS, a Registered Relocation Specialist, skilled in helping people quickly relocate across Canada to homes that are just right for them. He often receives referrals regarding executive relocations.

DiLiberto became licensed in the fall of 1988 and went to work for a year for a now defunct real estate firm that mainly conducted appraisals.

Eager to get into the sales side, he switched to Re/Max in 1989.

While he's sold investment and commercial properties and leased and sold shopping plazas, he prefers to focus primarily on residential real estate.

Challenging Start At Re/Max

DiLiberto's 1989 first year with Re/Max was a learning year in the midst of a booming market. The next year, 1990, mortgage rates shot up to 14 per cent.

"Suddenly, just as I was really getting going, the interest rates went up and activity slowed down to a crawl," he recalls, shaking his head.

"It made me improvise, take some marketing courses, and come up with alternative solutions. For example, I realized that people from out of town would likely appreciate our real estate values as they were paying more where they were." ,

iLiberto then launched some aggressive marke ing strategies to efficiently sell homes, including adver ising with real estate boards and publications i Oakville, Burlington and Mississauga.   He also contact d real estate agents i

these communities and got them to show their cli nts his listings offering far more house for the - dollars they were looking at spending.

As well, he developed target marketing to directly approach doctors, lawyers, dentists and other professionals in a position to buy the more expensive homes.

And he used multi-colour feature sheets to showcase his listings in a very attractive and professional manner.

He also accepted a broad array of listings in all price ranges and established himself as a regional realtor specializing in out-of-town buyers and investors.

Numerous Awards Of Merit

The bold strategy paid off: The same year, he was awarded the Platinum Club, recognizing sales achievement based on highest dollar value earned.

He's gone on to win Platinum Club distinction every year since.

Within four years of joining Re/Max, he was inducted into the Re/Max Hall Of Fame for earning more than $1-million over a four-year time span.

DiLiberto also won the Lifetime Achievement Award recognizing high sales volume over the 10-year period.

He's also ranked in the top 50 Re/Max agents of the more than 10,000 Re/Max agents across Canada, placing him in the organization's top 1 per cent.

And he's usually in the top 10 of more than 1,800 sales reps in the Metropolitan Hamilton Real Estate Board.

He does around 100 to 200 sales a year and it's a complete mix of homes, ranging from $64,000 to more than $1-million and adding up to many millions of dollars in total value.

Not that DiLiberto gets to keep all the real estate commissions he generates. Only a portion of the commission goes to him. And, as a self-employed realtor, he must cover the costs of his vehicle gas and maintenance; office space and phone; advertising; office administration; business cards; feature sheets and other expenses.

In 1992, he approached Re/Max to buy the West Hamilton franchise. Fortunately, that didn't work out as DiLiberto realized he'd rather work directly with people than serve as an administrator.

Appreciates Colleagues

"I enjoy working at Re/Max Escarpment Realty because the people there are all top producers and there's a high volume of sales and activity all the time," DiLiberto asserts, noting that he appreciates the work of other agents, even from other brokerages, in helping sell his listings. Many agents have been taken out to dinner or have received thank you plaques or gift certificates.

Proven Hands-on Approach

His hands-on approach includes spending uninterrupted time with clients and assessing their needs and financial capabilities concerning a home purchase. He also rotates real estate ads in several different publications to maximize property exposure for the vendor.

"I like working with people," DiLiberto asserts. "I keep in touch and keep them well informed."

He says clients appreciate the extra care and effort he brings. "People are usually pleased with the follow-up work we do. We'll send vendors reports, updates and newsletters to keep them apprised of where their home is being shown and the response it's getting."

Many Services Offered

DiLiberto also provides purchasers with a list of tips for making a wise buy.

He also provides house-showing tips and remodel-versus-sell comparisons.

As well, he provides a step-by-step guide for selling one's home with a check list so that matters such as final property tax and hydro payments etc. are not forgotten.

He also provides after-sale tips of things to watch out for after you've sold and moved into your new home.

And he shares market activity reports and newspaper articles to inform clients if the market is going up or down, what house types are selling the most and what locations are drawing the most interest from purchasers.

Special Deal With The Brick

He's also used his high-volume sales clout to benefit homebuyers.

DiLiberto made an arrangement with The Brick furniture stores to provide his clients with the opportunity to buy furniture, appliances and electronics at builder/contractor prices for their new home.

"I've been in real estate 15 years now and I still love it," DiLiberto asserts.

"I could job out more of the work, but I'd rather continue actively serving my clients – with Adele's assistance."

Credits Adele For Success

Indeed, while he's very much a hands-on realtor with direct involvement, DiLiberto also makes it clear that he's part of a close-knit, two-person team.

He credits his wife Adele, also a licensed real estate sales representative, for keeping him organized and focused on the client and for handling his calls and appointments.

"Adele is wonderful," he beams. "She keeps me well organized and on top of everything."

"Although she's licensed too," he continues, "rather than both of us selling, she concentrates on our services. She takes most of the phone calls, arranges appointments, sorts out my schedule, sets up open houses, sends out reports to clients regarding our advertising efforts, places ads, gets customer feedback, and generally does a lot of the behind-the-scenes work."

As DiLiberto notes: "Adele gives me time to show homes and spend time with clients," he says.

"It means if you call me, one of us will call back within an hour and make arrangements to serve you. It also means I can focus on you without interruptions."

Client Gets VIP Attention

Although he's frequently paged and receives at least 60 phone calls a day, DiLiberto does not interrupt his time with a client to take these calls.

For example, during the course of a lengthy interview, DiLiberto did not receive a single phone call – they were all handled by Adele.

"I like to focus just on the people I'm meeting with and talk to them one-to-one without disrupting things by taking phone calls, so Adele takes the calls and I return them when I've wrapped up with my client," he explains.

The result: Clients enjoy and appreciate his undivided attention free from any interruptions.

All of this help allows DiLiberto to focus on providing attentive care and service to his clients.

And DiLiberto is constantly seeking out new ways he can better service his clients.

"I'm a firm believer in continuing education and life-long learning," he states.

"I'm always looking for ways I can improve myself and increase my knowledge so I can do a better job serving the customers – there's always room for improvement."

Strong Community Supporter

DiLiberto is a strong community supporter who believes in helping the less-fortunate.

For example, his costly advertising on around 60 DARTS (Disabled Regional Transit System) buses provides considerable revenue for this worthy organization, supporting and improving the lives of handicapped people.

"It's a considerable cost," DiLiberto admits.

"But I know it's helping them an that's very important to me," he explains. "It's necessary and important to support and give back as much as you can to your community."

Endorsements And Referrals

Although some agents simply avoid private sellers entirely, DiLiberto makes a point of graciously and respectfully offering his expert services should the seller become frustrated (as is often the case) in their own sales efforts.

The low-key approach works wonders and has resulted in many referrals. Private sellers Stephen and Margaret Nichols wrote a sincere letter of endorsement praising DiLiberto for going out of his way to offer "the most constructive help and persistent interest in how we were progressing."

The Nichols were clearly impressed, adding: "He showed himself to be a professional in every way and when we did decide to list, we chose to list with him… he was able to secure an acceptable offer to purchase less than three weeks from date of listing."

Not surprisingly, DiLiberto finds much of his sales growth is from referrals from one satisfied homebuyer or seller recommending his services to others. One friend tells another friend who tells another friend who in turn keeps the referral process going.

Aggressive Marketing

DiLiberto has achieved considerable success through aggressive marketing – actually targeting and approaching key markets and potential buyers; along with an advertising strategy that rotates ads through a series of prominent real estate publications.

Another factor driving DiLiberto's success is his superb ability to negotiate deals. His marketing, negotiating and people skills obviously work: He's successfully negotiated more than $100-million in sales over the course of his 15 years in real estate.

Negotiating Skills

And his negotiating skills are all the more effective due to his adherence to the old Boy Scouts motto: Be Prepared.

"I really pride myself in being very thorough, in knowing the parties on both sides of the deal, their needs and wants, concerns and financial capabilities," DiLiberto says of his renowned negotiating skills. "I try to find the common ground, work out any problems that arise and bring the people together to make the deal happen."

To get to that point, DiLiberto does a lot of research to prepare himself for the offer presentation.

He anticipates questions and prepares answers in advance of queries being raised. The result: Deals are reached that take all circumstances into account; deals are struck that work well for all of the parties concerned. The deals are truly win-win situations.

House Came With A Jag

DiLiberto's pleasantly aggressive marketing approach was made famous by Street Beat columnist Paul Wilson in the pages of The Hamilton Spectator back in the mid-1990s.

Wilson invited Spectator readers to tag along with him on a visit to one of DiLiberto's listings, a home on Honeysuckle Crescent in Ancaster.

"Don't be shy," Wilson advised Street Beat readers. "There's a nice man waiting inside. His name is John DiLiberto and he's a real estate agent. He's going to show us the gleaming hardwood floors, the step-up Roman tub, the raised deck, the ensuites, the 2,800-square-feet of executive comfort."

Recognizing DiLiberto's salesmanship skills in what was then a difficult and slow market, Wilson added: "And he will make us feel we need to call this place our own."

Wilson went on to note the house, once valued

at $400,000 was now reduced in price to just $279,888 and, it came with a jet black, 1989 Jaguar Sovereign valued at more than $70,000.

The imaginative deal had captured the interest of a prominent newspaper columnist and his following.

Needless to say, the house sold. Someone became the proud owner of a very nice house – and a Jag. And John DiLiberto had made another sale.

Putting Deals Together

It was a win-win situation all round. But it wouldn't have happened at all had DiLiberto not had the marketing moxy to contact the media, generate exposure and draw the attention of qualified buyers.

Then he worked out all the details, structured an agreement and made the deal happen.

It was one of the more unusual real estate deals he's ever done, but in truth, he loves them all.

"I truly enjoy this work," DiLiberto says. "I find there's a lot of satisfaction in helping people deal with such a major transaction and life change."

"And most of all, I simply enjoy meeting and getting to know the people I come in contact with."

John DiLiberto's Tips For Success

1. Be very prepared when presenting information of any kind. Attention to detail makes a difference.

2. Do your homework. Research your subject whether it's the real estate market or another field.

3. Make your marketing efforts aggressive, high energy campaigns that draw attention and get results.

4. Don't reinvent the wheel. Borrow great ideas that work and make them your own.

5. Learn from others. Experience and expertise of those around you is a rich resource.

6. Concentrate on the job at hand. Focus on one task at a time to achieve success.

7. Consider a wide array of options and every opportunity. Don't limit your horizons.

8. Keep your customers informed and involved so they work with you to achieve a common goal.

9. Believe in life-long learning. Try to constantly increase your education and improve yourself.

10. Support your community in any way you can. It's important to give back to society.

Dr. Antonio Mancuso

Dr. Antonio Mancuso

Creating Perfect Smiles

"People want to have a great smile, and in the past few years we've seen a huge emphasis put on cosmetic dentistry."

- Dr. Antonio Mancuso

At a Glance:
Dr. Antonio Mancuso, dentist:

Dr. Antonio Mancuso, D.D.S, F.A.G.D.

Age: 44

Title: Dentist with private practice in Welland, Ont., President of the Ontario Academy Of General Dentistry and has served on the membership council of the national academy. Founder of the Millennium Aesthetics in Niagara Program. He's a fellow of the Academy of General Dentistry; fellow of the Academy of Dentistry International; fellow of the Pierre Fauchard Academy and a member of the American Academy of Cosmetic Dentistry.

Claim to fame: Dr. Mancuso is a leader in the field of cosmetic and aesthetic dentistry. He serves on numerous boards and organizations and organizes dental continuing education programs.

Personal: Resides in the Fonthill area of Pelham, near Welland, Ontario, with his wife Debby. Children include: Sarah, 18; Derek, 17; Caitlin, 11; and Matthew, 9. His practice is in Welland.

For More information:

Contact: Dr. Antonio Mancuso, Dentist.
(905) 734-9901. Toll free: 1-877-734-9901.
Fax: (905) 734-9993.
Address: 184 Thorold Rd W, Welland, Ont. L3C 3V7.
E-mail: tmancuso@cogeco.ca.
Website: www.millenniumaesthetics.com

Chapter Four

Dr. Antonio Mancuso

Creating Perfect Smiles

Success is more readily attainable if you meet life's challenges with a healthy, perfect smile.

A disarming smile can defuse an awkward, high-pressure situation. It expresses friendliness, confidence and self-assurance.

Flashing a perfect smile casts an image of youth, vitality and good physical health. And it sends a clear message that everything's fine and under control.

It's why so many successful people boast an engaging, confidence-building grin.

Welland dentist Dr. Antonio Mancuso is strong advocate of making your pearly whites as healthy and perfect as possible.

Dr. Mancuso's dental practice and his Millennium Aesthetics in Niagara program logo is: "The Creation Of The Perfect Smile," the words encircling a close-up image of that section of Michelangelo's 'The Creation' painting on the Sistine Chapel in Rome that depicts God's hand touching Adam's.

Indeed, when it comes to building great smiles, Dr. Mancuso puts his method where his mouth is.

"You can see from our logo the importance we place on a perfect smile" the Welland dentist grins, his mouth widening into a full, perfectly white smile.

Missing from his open-mouth smile is any trace of silver fillings. All you see are natural looking white teeth.

The reason quickly becomes apparent. Dr. Mancuso, 44, has undergone the same method of dentistry he applies to patients: His fillings, like their fillings, are of white porcelain.

His Own Fillings Are Porcelain

"I've had over ten of my own fillings done this way and I no longer like to do the mercury or silver fillings," he explains in an interview at his home in the nearby Fonthill community in Pelham where he resides with his wife Debby. Children include: Sarah, 18; Derek, 17; Caitlin, 11; and Matthew, 9.

"Porcelain fillings are much better," Dr. Mancuso continues, "because they're bonded into the tooth with a chemical adhesive which holds the tooth together – and they look natural."

Although a porcelain filling is about four times more costly than silver, Dr. Mancuso finds the advantages of porcelain are well worth the higher price: Porcelain fillings are very durable, trouble-free and attractive.

"It's very normal for me to do porcelain veneers on an 80-year-old patient," he notes.

"They should enjoy their last years on this earth and if they want to spend those years looking good, that's terrific."

"Aesthetic dentistry is very gratifying," Dr. Mancuso states.

"The patients really appreciate the work that's done on their behalf," he adds.

"I'll never forget the time I improved the smile of an 80-year-old lady," he grins.

"When she got out of the chair, she flashed me a big smile and said I'd changed her life. I can't tell you how good that makes me feel."

The growing popularity of porcelain fillings and veneers is part of a wider trend of consumers opting for services related to cosmetic dentistry.

Emphasis On Cosmetic Dentistry

Faced with a growing practice, Dr. Mancuso is now looking at leaving his Thorold Road location of 13 years to purchase his own unit – about 3,000 square feet – in a 9,000-square-foot medical professionals building that will house an eye doctor, dentists and a denture therapist.

"We're really cramped for space right now," he explains. "This will give us room to grow and the nice thing is, all of the space is on one floor for better organization."

The move will provide him with about 50 per cent more space and allow him to concentrate further on offering cosmetic dentistry services.

"I still have a family practice and I provide all the traditional dental services, from check-ups to root canals," Dr. Mancuso notes, "but the emphasis is on cosmetic dentistry."

"In fact," he adds, "nearly everything I do now has elements of cosmetic dentistry associated with it."

Mancuso attributes the rise in cosmetic dentistry popularity to demographics and societal trends.

"The baby boomers want the California smile and vibrant health," he explains.

"They want their teeth to look good and to feel good for a very long time."

Wants-Based Dentistry

Mancuso believes one of the biggest societal trends shaping dental practices is the pronounced shift from needs-based dentistry to what he describes as "wants-based dentistry."

"In the past, there was far less emphasis on prevention of cavities," he recalls.

"People didn't take care of their teeth to the extent many do now and a trip to the dentist tended to be out of necessity to see to a tooth ache," he points out.

"Now, there's quite a different phenomenon at work," Dr. Mancuso asserts.

"Now we see people opt for dental procedures that are wants-based and designed primarily to improve and enhance the appearance of their teeth," he adds.

"People want to have a great smile," Dr. Mancuso explains, "and in the past few years we've seen a huge emphasis put on cosmetic dentistry."

"From what I understand, some service industries won't even hire you unless you've got a great smile and smile a lot."

A Leader In Cosmetic Dentistry

Among the innovations employed at his practice is the use of argon lasers to affix fillings and apply laser whitening.

Dr. Mancuso also uses computer software to digitally depict how a patient's teeth will look after a procedure.

"When patients get an advance look at results, it gives them confidence in the process," explains Dr. Mancuso who has taught the scientific and artistic merits of smile design at seminars.

Indeed, Dr. Mancuso is a leader in the field of cosmetic and aesthetic dentistry.

He serves on numerous boards and organizations and organizes dental continuing education programs devised and designed to help take the profession of dentistry to ever higher levels.

Among his many distinctions, Dr. Mancuso is president of the prestigious Ontario Academy of General Dentistry and he has served on the membership council of the national academy.

He is also on the editorial board for Spectrum/ CJDT journal, circulated to dentists and dental technologists across Canada and the United States.

He has had numerous articles published in this and other dental journals.

Founder Of Millennium Aesthetics

He's also founder of Millennium Aesthetics in Niagara and organizes intensive programs to enable fellow dentists to transform their dental practices to reflect the changing needs and wants of their patients.

Dr. Mancuso founded Millennium Aesthetics in Niagara in 1999 after the University of Toronto discontinued the course in aesthetic dentistry that he'd been an instructor in.

"I felt it was important to share information and new technologies and I decided to take this on and to continue to raise the bar for the Canadian aesthetic dentists," Dr. Mancuso states.

"I teamed up with other prominent aesthetic dentists to create an educational experience in which the whole is greater than the sum of its parts. We've now done five of these courses – and each time it keeps getting bigger and better."

Dr. Mancuso performs a number of roles in organizing and presenting the live, hands-on Millennium Aesthetics program.

He serves as the Millennium Aesthetics program course director, expert speaker, instructor and master of ceremonies.

Hands-on Program

And he continues to be heavily involved in his hands-on Millennium Aesthetics company boasting his artistic 'The Creation Of The Perfect Smile' logo.

Once a year, he runs an extensive program on smile makeovers in which the participating dentists bring in a dental patient at Niagara College and perform work on this patient, under the supervision of Dr. Mancuso and his faculty who demonstrate the latest techniques and procedures.

As course director, Dr. Mancuso also teaches seminars and delivers formal lectures at a local hotel. And he introduces other expert instructors and speakers during conventions he personally organizes.

Conceived and developed by Dr. Mancuso, The Millennium Aesthetics in Niagara live, hands-on program teaches dentists and staff anterior aesthetic diagnosis and treatment.

Coursework covers the latest leading-edge aesthetic techniques, applications and procedures.

It can also cover adhesive dentistry, top steps to integrate aesthetics into any dental practice, leading critical diagnostic skills, superior restorations, and new non-orthodontic procedures.

And it always offers a close look at the latest promising developments in dental technology.

Many Testimonials

The two-week programs are widely respected and valued by leading dentists across Ontario, many of whom are pleased to provide strong endorsements and testimonials:

Dr. Mark Lin of North York regards the program as indispensable: This course is a must for anyone serious about cosmetic dentistry," he states.

"The best hands-on course available in Canada… invaluable to anyone planning on practicing dentistry seriously," asserts Dr. K. Khaled of Mississauga.

"If you are not doing this kind of dentistry, you are missing out on opportunities for you and your patients…" states yet another dentist from Nova Scotia, Dr. J. G. Violette.

And Dr. Matt Muisiner of Kingston offers these words of praise: "Millennium Aesthetics provided me and my team a blueprint as to how to incorporate aesthetic dentistry into my practice. I have never attended a more comprehensive, well-organized program."

"The principles taught in the course are not only relevant to the larger cases, but can be applied to everyday dentistry," acknowledges Dr. Bruce Mansbridge of Stoney Creek.

"My level of enthusiasm is ever higher than the first time I took this course because now I know from experience that what I've been taught really works," attests Judy Wagner, treatment co-ordinator for Dr. Doug Jones of Waterloo.

Lisa Philp, president of Transitions Consulting Group, deems the program "nothing short of spectacular in regards to evidence based content and delivery… your course provides a positive learning environment, and allowed the participants to filter the expert advice of all instructors and customize it to their individual philosophy… providing them with the technical confidence to be successful in smile design."

And that's just a few of the many testimonials volunteered by attendees at Millennium Aesthetics conferences held at Dr. Mancuso's scenic hometown of

Niagara Falls, Ontario, the honeymoon capital of the world and home to one of nature's greatest wonders.

Recognized Dentistry Expert

In addition to Millennium-related speaking engagements, Dr. Mancuso has emerged as an expert in the field of dentistry and has given lectures to dental organizations in Canada and the United States; taught courses in aesthetic dentistry; contributed articles to local newspapers, industry publications and dental journals; and has appeared on television programs, including Canada AM.

The burgeoning added attention has prompted a major adjustment in the normally low-key dentist's life.

"Prior to 1999, I'd never written an article, I'd never given a formal lecture and I'd never run a large organization," he says with a chuckle.

"Now all of that is such a big part of my life," he adds, noting that he's delivered more than 150 lectures and speaking engagements since 1999 and has a full slate of engagements ahead of him that will take him well into 2004.

President of Ontario Academy

As well, Dr. Mancuso is president of the Ontario Academy of General Dentistry and a fellow of the Academy. With Dr. Mancuso at the helm, the Ontario AGD has experienced an impressive 30 per cent annual growth in membership rates and now boasts nearly 800 members, making it one of the fastest-growing academies in North America.

He's also a fellow of the Academy of Dentistry International; a fellow of the Pierre Fauchard Academy and member of the American Academy of Cosmetic Dentistry and numerous other organizations.

Simply put, he's the go-to guy that dentists turn to when they want expert advice on running a successful practice emphasizing cosmetic dentistry.

Modest Beginnings

How Dr. Mancuso rose to such heights in the dental field is a story that begins in a small town outside of Catanzaro, Calabria in southern Italy – and it's here that we find some of the underlying reasons for his drive and ambition.

In 1959, Filippo Mancuso and his wife Gina welcomed the arrival of Antonio and two years later, his sister, Josephine.

The close-knit family lived in an impoverished rural community.

"My parents were farm labourers on someone else's farm – they made barely enough to put food on the table," Dr. Mancuso recalls.

"We lived on the farm in the summer and lived in the town of Sorbo S. Basile – a two-hour hike – in the winter because, unlike the farm, it had electricity.

Importance Of Family Values

"We were very poor, but I didn't know we were poor because we had family," Dr. Mancuso smiles, "and family is everything – anything else is secondary – that's been bred into me from childhood."

"Besides," he continues, "we had fun on the farm, chasing the farm animals and just enjoying childhood. I still remember sitting on a cold ceramic floor with a bunch of other wide-eyed kids watching the only black-and-white TV in town – it was the early 1960s."

It was also during the early 1960s that Dr. Mancuso's father went to Canada and Niagara Falls to work as a labourer for a Gerber's Baby Food plant.

The rest of the family joined him in the fall of 1966 and by the end of the decade, the parents had purchased their first home, across the street from the Niagara Falls Arena, on Lewis Avenue.

Inspired By Parents' Sacrifice

"I'm always inspired by my parents – they were so hard-working," Dr. Mancuso says, shaking his head.

"My dad worked as a labourer, my mom worked as a chambermaid, long hours for little pay. I can't fathom what they must have gone through, coming over to a new country with no skills, no language, and supporting a family. It must have been very tough, an incredible shock to the system, but they did it – and they did it all for their children."

"And I didn't want to ever let them down," he continues, "so I put pressure on myself to succeed, for them, to get marks in school and excel."

Period of Adjustment

The Mancusos' first-born son also went through his own period of adjustment.

"As a young boy, I loved the falls and Canada and

I was an avid soccer player – still am in fact. But I hated the winter, the cold – the most we got in southern Italy was a few flurries. Language was a big adjustment too. I felt like it was taking forever for me to learn English, but it wasn't. Kid's minds are like sponges, they soak everything up and I was speaking English in no time."

A second sister, Rosa was born in 1973. "Mom would take me, Josephine and Rosa to work with her and we'd clean motel rooms because she couldn't afford a baby-sitter," Dr. Mancuso recalls.

"Although my parents learned to speak English, they couldn't read it, so as a nine-year-old, I'd read their mail aloud to them," he recalls.

"I had no idea what I was reading sometimes, due to a nine-year-old's limited vocabulary – but I was happy that I could do something for them for a change."

Excelled At School

The future dentist continued to excel at school. After graduating from high school with A-plus grades and a number of academic awards, he studied Natural Sciences at the University of Western Ontario.

That program normally leads to the medical field and his goal at that time was to become a medical doctor.

Fateful Toothache

Then, fate intervened in the form of a toothache.

"An upper wisdom tooth was cutting through the gums – it was painful," Dr. Mancuso recalls.

"Someone noticed my pain and directed me to a dental clinic on campus," he recollects.

"I had no idea the clinic existed but I was very impressed with these young kids in white smocks," he adds, shaking his head at the memory.

"They took very good care of me. They took the tooth out painlessly and did terrific follow-up work. That's when I realized this is what I wanted to do. Until then I'd never even thought about a career in dentistry. I applied right away and was accepted."

Dr. Mancuso says he still achieved his goal of earning his parents' pride.

"I was still in the medical field. But as a dentist, I wasn't on call for the most part," he notes.

"And, I didn't have to worry about getting called in on an emergency. I had more time for family and soccer and a social life. I could live a balanced life – it was really an odd twist of fate, but it turned out to be a great career choice."

He went on to study dentistry at the University of Toronto faculty of dentistry for four years, graduating from U of T in 1985. He's maintained a dental practice in Welland ever since.

Chooses Welland

Why Welland? Right from the start of his career, he's understood the important role that demographics play in dentistry.

Although he was raised in the city of Niagara Falls, Dr. Mancuso decided to set up practice in neighbouring Welland largely due to demographic trends in the Rose City.

"I researched the demographics and found a lot of older dentists who would soon retire," he recalls.

In 1987, Dr. Mancuso purchased an established dental practice from a retiring dentist and then merged it with his own Thorold Road, Welland practice.

By 1990, Dr. Mancuso's practice had grown to such an extent that he needed substantially more space.

He moved a few blocks down Thorold Road to his existing location: a century-plus older home with a major addition.

He now has about 2,000 square feet of space on the main floor, with second level offices and basement level staff lounge and laboratories.

A contemplated new location in Welland would provide him with 3,000 square feet of space on one floor.

Thriving Practice

The thriving practice provides the progressive dentist with a strong source of professional satisfaction.

Dr. Mancuso's staff has grown in leaps and bounds. Including him, it now numbers 14, also including three hygienists, three administrators, three assistants, a denture therapist and an associate.

His 76-year-old father-in-law, Dr. Tony Tulumello, also a dentist, drops in each week to work on patients.

And Dr. Mancuso's wife Debby also comes into the office one day a week to help out with administrative work, including handling the Millennium Aesthetics administrative chores.

"We're just one big happy family," Dr. Mancuso says playfully as cheerful staff members chuckle.

Then he strikes a more serious note: "You know, teamwork is one of those important aspects of our lives that are all too often forgotten in the grind of everyday living. But without teamwork, even the most gifted dentist would not be as successful at carrying out his/her craft. We need to acknowledge our team – and I certainly do – and thank them for all they do for our success. They make our success possible."

Dr. Mancuso has learned many other valuable life lessons along the way.

"I've learned to practice the mantra of being firm in principle but flexible in practice," he asserts. "For example, I'm firm that a task must be done, but flexible as to how it's done."

"As well," he continues, "I've learned that if you truly want to master something, teach it."

"For example I've been coaching soccer since I was 18-years-old and I found that in order to coach, I had to thoroughly understand the game. For me to teach other dentists, I must first understand the principles myself. This approach helps you organize your thoughts."

Plays To His Strengths

Dr. Mancuso has also learned to play to his strengths, concentrating on dentistry while bringing in practice-management specialists to manage his office.

"Schools teach us how to be dentists, but not how to run a successful practice – there's no management or small business training, so it makes sense to turn to people who have those skills rather than try to reinvent the wheel," he says.

"The day you graduate is the day your formal education is finished, but education is a life-long process and I need to stay current in dentistry," adds Dr. Mancuso, who also enjoys reading a lot of self-help and self-improvement books and begins his day reading motivational quotes.

"I remember being almost ready to quit dental school because I found I had such a heavy workload and tons of reading. Then, after I graduated, I became a course-junkie – I could go courses because they weren't compulsory now – they were fun."

Much of Dr. Mancuso's practice growth is built on referrals.

"I fall into the old 20-80 rule as 20 per cent of my clientele provides 80 per cent of my business and I know I should target this group," he points out.

"But I'm Canadian and proud of it – so I'm not flashy. I like to take a low-key approach of asking for referrals from this target group."

Technological Advancements

Dr. Mancuso finds many of the new technological advancements in dentistry are simply awe-inspiring.

"We can now get precise, computerized measurements of the muscles in your face and readings in terms of elasticity and muscle tone – this is a real breakthrough in neuromuscular dentistry, which emphasizes making the facial muscles comfortable so the teeth will also work well in chewing and other functions," he explains.

"The technology has changed the way we do dentistry – and it's all very much to the benefit of the patient who now spends a lot less time in the dentist's chair to get the best treatment possible."

Dr. Mancuso anticipates he'll continue to invest in new technology and explore new dentistry approaches well into the new millennium.

For example, he recently invested $163,000 for a cad/cam (computer assisted design/computer assisted manufacturing) machine that employs a computerized milling system for the making of crowns as well as porcelain tooth restorations.

"With this machine, it's done in one appointment only, one less visit than the patient would normally face," Dr. Mancuso explains.

"This process eliminates the need to make an impression – now it's just an optical image that's taken – and the crown or restoration is designed by computer and milled right then and there in a matter of minutes. Then it's fitted into the patient's mouth. Done."

No Need To Make An Impression

Dr. Mancuso smiles and shakes his head. "Just think about that for a moment," he grins.

"The whole process takes an hour – literally half the time."

"But in fact," he continues, "it's really just a tiny fraction of the time compared with the old way of doing things, when you consider that there was a two-week wait in the past for the impression to be made."

Dr. Mancuso notes the new system is far more efficient and convenient for patients.

"And I guess I'm the kind of guy who doesn't really need to make an impression," he adds with a laugh.

He's also spent $10,000 US and $25,000 US on state-of-the-art lasers for the thorough laser-curing and whitening of teeth.

This also includes soft-tissue lasers that sculpt the gums and allow the tissue to heal quickly with little to no bleeding.

"I like to make extensive use of the available technological advancements to create greater benefit for the patients," Dr. Mancuso asserts.

"Why not make the visit to the dentist as brief, pleasant and pain-free as possible? People really appreciate the extra care."

Enjoys Family Life

When he's not practicing dentistry or involved in organizing and presenting seminars, Dr. Mancuso can be found enjoying his home-life in Niagara.

He ranks his top priorities in life, in order of importance, as family, his profession of dentistry, and soccer.

In fact, Dr. Mancuso has been an avid player and coach of amateur soccer teams for many years.

And he continues to couch youth soccer teams five days a week.

Three of his four children play soccer and he also plays in an old-timers soccer league.

"I love soccer," he beams.

"I don't have a cottage or boat, but put me on a soccer field and I'm in heaven. It's also a great family activity."

And Dr. Mancuso places a lot of importance on family life.

"I was raised believing family is everything and I still believe that to this day," he asserts.

"Family comes first, always has, always will. Family is what it's all about," he adds.

Dr. Mancuso recalls having tears in his eyes when he watched his daughter graduate in the auditorium of Niagara Falls Collegiate and Vocational Institute (the school building now houses an adult learning centre).

"That was my old high school – and now a new generation was taking the stage," he recollects, noting that 24 years earlier, he had also graduated, crossing the same stage to accept his diploma and awards for academic achievement.

"My father cried because he was caught up in the emotional experience of seeing me graduate… now my own daughter was walking across the exact same stage to accept her diploma, her many awards and giving the valedictorian address. I had tears in my own eyes." he recalls fondly.

"I don't think there's any greater joy than seeing your children succeed and achieve great things – it makes all of life's struggles worthwhile. "

Dr. Antonio Mancuso's Tips For Success:

1. If you truly want to master something, teach it. To teach it, you must first fully understand it so thoroughly that you can instruct others.

2. Accept and embrace opportunity. When opportunity knocks, open the door.

3. Develop goals based on something you're good at and that you enjoy doing. Play to your strengths.

4. Think about what you want to achieve and set about making your dreams a reality.

5. Be fully rounded. Excel in academics, but don't be a bookworm – get involved in sports or a physical activity and develop a social life for good mental and physical health.

6. Be firm in principle but flexible in practice. For example be firm that a task must be done, but flexible as to how it's done.

7. There's no substitute for hard work. Do your work with passion and enthusiasm to succeed.

8. Embrace life-long learning and the joy of always expanding your knowledge base.

9. Delegate: You can't do everything so focus on what you're best at and bring in experts to do the rest. Surround yourself with good people.

10. Play hard and work hard. The more you put into life, the more you'll get out.

11. Practice what you preach. Set an example for others. If you don't believe in yourself, how can you expect others to believe in you?

12. Don't reinvent the wheel. It's faster to copy perfection, learn the lessons of others and make them your own. Take an expert's approach and modify it to suit your own personality and objectives.

13. Change is a constant in life. Embrace change and all the opportunities and possibilities it provides for growth and improved efficiency.

14. It's one thing to do it right, it's another to do the right thing. Balance your skills with ethics to ensure you deliver a treatment or service to someone that's right for them.

Sam Mercanti

Chapter 5

CARSTAR
Automotive

Star Treatment For You And Your Vehicle

"This is our starship location, where we'll develop new programs, new innovative ways to repair vehicles, faster, better, more efficiently and at less cost."

- Sam Mercanti

At a Glance:
CARSTAR Automotive:

Sam Mercanti
Age: 56
Title: CEO and President, CARSTAR

Claim to fame: Among the many distinctions earned by Mercanti and his CARSTAR team are ISO 9000 status from the International Standards Organization; the Hamilton Chamber of Commerce Outstanding Business Achievement Award – large company category – for the year 1990; the 1997 Collision Industry Pride Award – Mercanti is the first Canadian to ever win the prestigious American award. He's also been twice nominated for Entrepreneur of The Year (1995 and 1997) by Canadian Business magazine; and he's won the Spirit Of The Community Award from the Hamilton Safe Communities Coalition. As well, CARSTAR has been ranked among the top 200 fastest growing companies in Canada by Profit magazine.

Financial Data: Annual sales approach $100-million and the company is growing steadily.

Personal: Resides in Hamilton with wife Roma and the couple have three daughters: Lisa, 31; Jennifer, 27; and Samantha, 22.
For More information: Contact Sam Mercanti:
(905) 388-4720. Fax: (905) 388-1124
Address: 2nd-1124 Rymal Road East., Hamilton, Ontario, L8W 3N7.
Email: smercanti@carstar.ca

Chapter 5

CARSTAR Automotive

Star Treatment For You And Your Vehicle

Sam Mercanti has envisioned the future of the auto collision repair industry – and StarPlex is a bold statement of what's to come.

Mercanti, president and CEO of CARSTAR Automotive Canada, beams with pride as he gazes at the StarPlex, a 25,000-square-foot, state-of-the-art, collision repair centre.

"StarPlex provides the next level of customer service – which we call 'Star Treatment' – and it will ultimately also drive progress in every aspect of the

CARSTAR mission," Mercanti, 56, asserts, motioning toward the impressive structure on a 3.2-acre site on Argentia Road in Mississauga.

"It will deliver the highest level of cost containment, improved turnaround times and client retention for our insurance partners," he adds as he takes in the sight of the sprawling $5-million facility, next to the Shell Service Centre, between Winston Churchill Boulevard and Erin Mills Parkway.

StarPlex State-Of-The-Art

"The StarPlex is a brand new collision repair centre with state-of-the-art functionality, including modern technology and innovative and highly efficient management systems," Mercanti says of the complex near Highway 401 in Mississauga's fast-growing Meadowvale community, projected to have a population of about 200,000 people by 2005.

"It's like the Home Depot of collision centres – it's the first retail driven collision centre in Canada where customers enjoy the ultimate collision repair experience," adds Mercanti, whose trademark slogan for the forerunner Ontario Auto Collision – "A bang-up job every time," – remains a familiar phrase for many Canadians.

Mercanti says the industry average for collision repair turnaround – how long it takes for repairs to be completed and you get your vehicle back – is 11 days, while at CARSTAR, it's just 7 days. Not satisfied with this level of performance, he wants to reduce the turnaround time to just under five days.

"We want to drive out inefficiencies and

establish the best practices across Canada," he notes.

"We've hired process engineers to identify any inefficiencies in repairing a vehicle, from collision to completion of repairs. At this facility we'll do some teaching and demonstrate to franchisees how to adopt best practices," he continues.

"This is our starship location," he adds, "and it's where we'll develop new programs, new innovative ways to repair vehicles, faster, better, more efficiently and at less cost."

It's also the latest initiative for the industry-leading CARSTAR company, which now boasts nearly 100 locations across Canada that collectively generate more than $100-million in annual sales.

Mercanti Credits Others

Mercanti credits CARSTAR's impressive success to the combined efforts of the various location managers; suppliers; insurance partners; CARSTAR staff; and his founding partners: uncles Nardino, Guerino and Anthony Mercanti; along with a talented executive, which includes Larry Jeffries, executive vice-president of franchise operations; and Sam Malatesta, senior vice-president of CARSTAR Automotive Canada.

Malatesta, who also handles much of the company's marketing, says CARSTAR is recognizing marketplace trends and positioning itself to take advantage of consumer preferences with the new STARPLEX facility.

"There is a general trend towards the big-box format as shopping patterns continue to shift towards the outskirts of larger urban centres," Malatesta notes. "We are seeing this in all types of industries, including grocery stores, hardware stores, bookstores – and now our own stores."

"The goal," he adds, "is to expand… in order to drive more volume in the stores – ultimately, the belief is that the big will get bigger, the smaller will get more niche-oriented and specialized and anything in between is going to disappear."

Benchmark Services

Malatesta notes the STARPLEX offers a number of benchmark services, including: 8 am to 8 pm hours of multi-shift operation, seven days a week; lifetime nation-wide warranties; VIP pickup and delivery shuttle services; on-site car rental agency; interior and exterior detailing with every repair; and 24-hour accident assistance and towing services.

"We expect to have faster repair times that will lower car rental and administrative costs." he notes.

"The store will also be both ISO 9001 and CQS9000 registered, which validates all internal operational/management processes. We'll incorporate quality control processes that reduce defects to less than 1 per cent defect. And we'll offer all of this using the new, highly efficient CARSTAR Operating System to manage information and data bases, which in turn should enable the insurers to be more profitable through better risk management."

Malatesta lauds Mercanti's entrepreneurial spirit: "Just as Home Depot, Famous Players and Canadian Tire have transformed their respective industries, Sam Mercanti has envisioned this location to be the future of the collision repair industry."

Indeed it's Mercanti's vision that has guided this business through each stage of its corporate evolution. His hands-on management style continues to drive CARSTAR to new levels of success.

Numerous Awards

Among the many distinctions earned by Mercanti and his CARSTAR team are ISO 9000 status from the International Standards Organization; the Hamilton Chamber of Commerce Outstanding Business Achievement Award – large company category – for the year 1990; the 1997 Collision Industry Pride Award – Mercanti is the first Canadian to ever win the prestigious American award.

He's also been twice nominated for Entrepreneur of The Year (1995 and 1997) by Canadian Business magazine; and he's won the Spirit Of The Community Award from the Hamilton Safe Communities Coalition. As well, CARSTAR has been ranked among the top 200 fastest growing companies in Canada by Profit magazine.

Active Community Supporter

Mercanti has long been active in assisting the community, helping many worthy causes.

Beyond his support for the Safe Communities Coalition, he sits on the board of trustees for St. Joseph's Hospital in Hamilton.

He's also spent more than a decade as the

chairman of the advisory committee for the Centre For Ambulatory Health Services in Stoney Creek.

As well, Mercanti heads a Christian men's self-improvement group aimed at creating better husbands, fathers and businessmen.

How CARSTAR Automotive Canada and Sam Mercanti achieved such enviable success is a story that has its beginnings in a small town in Italy.

Born In Italy

Sam Mercanti, now 56, was born Sept. 14, 1947, to Giuseppe and Iolanda Mercanti in the scenic village of Castelli, in the mountainous Abruzzo region of north-central Italy.

He was the eldest of four children and would soon be joined by his brothers Peter, now 54, and Morris, now 50, while their sister Rosanna, now 40, would be born in Canada.

The picturesque village is situated on a rocky plateau in the shadow of snow-capped mountains.

Approximately a two-hour drive from Rome, the community is famous for its Castellian ceramics, drawing throngs of tourists eager to buy hand-made ceramic pottery, tiles and works of art and travel through the scenic surrounding farmlands.

Despite the idyllic setting, life was less than ideal for the young family in the quaint community of less than 2,000 people.

Parents Sharecroppers

"My parents were sharecroppers, farmers who didn't own any land and it wasn't easy for them to provide for a whole family on what they received from their work," Mercanti explains.

"My family's ties went back forever in the little town and I can remember going to school there and how hilly the area was," he continues. "I can also remember drawing water from a mountain cave – and when I went back for a visit, decades later, I found the farm was abandoned and the cave opening grown-over, but once I cleared the bramble there was the well and the water was still cold and refreshing."

"My parents worked on a hillside farm, about the size of a hobby farm. It was very hard to make a living. There was little opportunity for success in the community, so by the time I was nine-years-old, my parents had decided to move to Canada and Hamilton."

The Move To Canada

In 1956, the Mercanti family immigrated to Canada, arriving by ship at Pier 21 in Halifax. Then came the long train ride from Halifax to Hamilton's CN rail station at James Street North.

"My family was given two loaves of white bread during the train ride, and we thought it was cake – we never put sugar in bread in Italy, only salt," Mercanti recalls.

Despite other such adjustments to life in Canada, Mercanti has no regrets. Far from it.

"I thank God my parents decided to take us all to Canada, to take that risk, to leave their home of many generations for a new land of opportunity," Mercanti states, his voice catching in his throat.

"And I'm especially grateful they came to

Hamilton for the opportunities here. Some people say I've got an enterprising spirit – but that never existed until I came here. My parents gave us the opportunity to succeed. They did it all for their children."

His mother picked fruit on area farms while father initially worked as a construction labourer.

Then, in 1957, his father went to work for his third cousins, Frank and Ralph Mercanti, who had started the first Mercanti auto-body business in 1953 in the Bay and Vine streets area.

Half-Century Tradition

The Mercanti name has now been ingrained in this business for half a century.

"My dad usually prepped cars for paint jobs," Mercanti recalls, "and in the summer time, Dad would take me to work with him. He taught me how to prep cars and do detail work when I was 15 years old."

That was Sam Mercanti's introduction to the auto restoration business.

And at the same time, his entrepreneurial streak began to emerge.

Enterprising Youth

"My brothers and I would buy 20 copies of the Saturday afternoon edition of The Hamilton Spectator at 6 cents each and then run to the street corners and sell them for the full regular price of 10 cents a paper," he recalls with a smile.

"A lot of kids did the same thing – and if somebody took somebody else's corner there'd be fist-fights – it was very competitive."

But the Mercanti boys entrepreneurial drive didn't end with the quick profit derived from selling newspapers at nearly twice their bulk-purchased price.

Once the papers were sold, the brothers were off and running again, this time to the Hamilton Farmer's Market where they rushed up to a florist selling fresh-cut roses.

"The roses were cut fresh earlier in the day," Mercanti points out, "so by the time we got there, any unsold roses would soon be in danger of wilting."

Always willing to help out a florist in need, the Mercanti brothers struck a deal.

"We'd buy up their fresh-cut flowers for just 25 cents a bunch," Mercanti grins, "and then we'd stand outside the downtown hotels and sell them to the ladies' escorts for $1 a bunch.

Faced with an enterprising young man selling roses, a gentleman's only correct response was: Yes, he'd be delighted to buy roses for his lady friend.

"And we got tips," Mercanti laughs, shaking his head. "We'd head home Saturday night with $50 between the three of us. It was outrageous. Our dad was working for $1-an-hour and $40-a-week was an average wage. We got more than that between us in one night."

Valuable Lessons Learned

Mercanti learned some valuable lessons in the process. "We learned to buy low, sell high and be quick about it. And timing is everything: A day-old paper is worth nothing. Dead flowers are worth nothing. You have to hustle and move fast to seize opportunity."

And Mercanti's unquestionable enterprising spirit continued undiminished into high school.

While attending Westdale High, and then Central High schools, Mercanti became aware of another consumer need waiting to be filled.

"There weren't many dance halls in the area, especially for young people," he recalls. "So I decided to run my own dance hall. I talked to the owner of a pool room on James Street North at Wilson Street. The upstairs room was just sitting there empty, so he let me fix it up and use it as a dance hall and we split the earnings. We had great turn-outs. It was a lot of fun – and very profitable too."

Joins Auto Body Shop Business

In 1964, Mercanti, then 17-years-old and eager to continue seeking opportunities in the working world, dropped out of high school in Grade 10 and went to work for Mercanti Brothers Auto Body run by his uncles Nardino and Guerino Mercanti on Strachan Street.

"I started doing detail work and prepping cars for paint jobs," he recollects. "Then I got my technical body man's licence and I fixed cars."

In 1967, Mercanti found himself writing estimates. His uncles had some lingering difficulty reading and writing in English and the young nephew – then barely 20 – enjoyed working the front desk, writing estimates and dealing with customers.

The Mercanti brothers' auto body shop property was expropriated by the City of Hamilton in 1968 for civic development so they moved their business to a new location, opening shop on Gage Avenue North under the new name: Ontario Auto Collision.

At that time, a third uncle, Anthony Mercanti, came into the business and the growing shop needed a general manager. The uncles turned to their hard-working nephew, the one with the entrepreneurial spirit, the gift of the gab, the sales and marketing skills and the urge to run things. Sam Mercanti was moving up in the world.

In 1968, Ontario Auto Collision was then averaging $100 for some body work and a paint job on used vehicles. At that time, the bulk of the company's business was from used car and warranty jobs and only 5 per cent from insurance companies.

Insurance Claims Became Focus

"That same year," Mercanti says raising an eyebrow, "we had an insurance job come in – a 1966 black Pontiac – and this two-year-old car needed some work. It was a $1,100 job – eleven times what we were averaging with most jobs. It did need a little more body work and paint and parts. But we'd have to paint 11 cars to get that kind of money. And the insurance jobs are very stable – you're definitely going to get paid – and there's a better gross profit."

For Mercanti, the insurance job experience was nothing less than a revelation.

"I decided to go after the untapped insurance business and I met with brokers, agents and appraisers to assess their needs and earn their business," recalls Mercanti, who also succeeded in raising Ontario Auto Collision's consumer market presence with his famous marketing campaign and TV commercials promising "A bang-up job every time."

"The insurance industry was key," he adds. "I realized we needed to put our focus there, so I put together a sales force and we became the first auto body shop to have a sales force dedicated to bringing in business from insurance companies, insurance brokers and owners of fleets of vehicles."

Although Ontario Auto Collision continued to serve a wide clientele including people from all walks of life, it concentrated on bringing in insurance business.

The sharpened focus soon paid off: In 1968, Ontario Auto Collision was a $100,000-a-year business. In 1972, just four years later, it had grown to become a $1-million-a-year business. And insurance jobs accounted for 50 per cent of revenue. This explains why Mercanti is one of the few people who speaks of insurance firms with genuine affection, and in reverential tones usually reserved for sports heroes.

"A lot of thanks has to go to the insurance companies, they embraced me early on and the business relationship is very good," Mercanti asserts.

An Important Year

For Mercanti, 1972 was a pivotal year in more ways than one.

"I married Roma, the girl of my dreams," he says grinning widely. The couple have three daughters: Lisa, 31; Jennifer, 27; and Samantha, 22.

Also in 1972, with the company doing nearly a $1-million annually, Mercanti was getting restless and was contemplating opening up his own shop and going into business for himself.

After making his uncles aware of his thoughts, they realized there was only one thing to do: They made their nephew president of Ontario Auto Collision and a full partner with 25 per cent ownership of the business.

In 1978, Ontario Auto Collision crossed the $2-million-a-year revenue threshold and needed more room to accommodate its fleet of 10 vehicles and burgeoning business. It acquired neighbouring buildings and land for parking and expanded to include 10 service bays, a larger office and waiting room, and additional customer parking.

Next, the Bank of Montreal loaned Ontario Auto Collision its first $200,000 business development loan and the company built a 10,000-square-foot, state-of-the-art facility.

Multi-Million-Dollar Company

In 1982, the company was doing $3-million in annual sales and was developing a strong management team that came to include his cousin, Tony Mercanti, son of Guerino.

Ontario Auto Collision acquired the former McPetrie Motors Company in Burlington – the land, building, business and assets – and Mercanti took over its operations as manager. In two years it went from $400,000 in annual revenue to more than $1-million.

In 1987, Mercanti established Ontario Trucking Division for collision repairs to trucks and OAC opened its first Ontario Trucking Division store at a Gage Avenue location. The same year, Mercanti turned over the management of the Burlington location – renamed as Ontario Auto Collision – to another cousin, Dino Mercanti, the son of Nardino.

Also that same year, Mercanti established OAM (Ontario Auto Management) and he founded the property management arm GNAS (named for the partners: Guerino, Nardino, Anthony and Sam).

And, still in 1987, the company did another acquisition, buying the land and building for its Ontario Auto Collision location on Highway 53 in Ancaster. Sam Saputo, the production manager at the Burlington store, was transferred to the Ancaster store as general manager.

Headquarters Built

The following year came the 1988 acquisition of land on Highway 53 near Upper Ottawa Street on Hamilton Mountain. And in 1990, Ontario Auto Collision built its signature $5-million, 36,000-square-foot building housing its headquarters, an auto mall, body shop and 15,000 square feet of leased-out units.

Another cousin, Remo Mercanti, son of Guerino, was named corporate locations manager, while his brother Sam, another Sam Mercanti, managed one of the OAC locations.

In 1992, OAF (Ontario Auto Franchise) opened a location in Stoney Creek and put Domenic and Roseanna Lucarelli at the helm.

Running Out Of Mercantis

Lucarelli? "We were running out of Mercantis to manage locations," Mercanti shrugs with just the hint of a smile. "Domenic was the production manager at our head office site and he had plans to open either a body shop of his own or a catering business. I didn't

118

want to lose this guy – he's a great entrepreneur and a hard-worker – and I know how it is to be restless, so I helped him start-up the Stoney Creek franchise."

In 1993, The Ancaster location was franchised and was sold to managers Sam and Rosa Saputo.

That same year, Sam Malatesta, then an Honours student in the Business program at McMaster University, was brought in to handle sales, marketing and insurance relations. "His main job was to get cars to our door," Mercanti asserts.

The year 1993 marked the 10th anniversary of Mercanti's 1983 founding of a management system: CARS (Computerized Automotive Repairing System). It had provided a new organizational dimension to the business with consistent standards and business ethics at all locations.

In 1994, Ontario Auto Collision franchised its Burlington operation. OAC was by now a highly successful franchising company with eight locations across Ontario and $12-million in annual sales.

As well, Mercanti had by now made Ontario Auto Collision a household name with his famous "bang-up" slogan.

Industry Changing

Still, he detected dark clouds on the horizon.

"I saw the industry was changing, and usually when that happens, regional players get clobbered."

Mercanti looked south to the fast-growing CARSTAR auto collision repairs franchise company in the United States, which then boasted 360 locations in the U.S. After carefully examining the pros and cons of an alliance, Mercanti signed an agreement and acquired a master licensee agreement for all of Canada in 1995. He now had the exclusive right to open and license CARSTAR locations across Canada. This marked the start of CARSTAR Automotive Canada, and the beginning of many good things to come.

Next, Mercanti assembled a team, including Larry Jeffries from the giant BASF paint company, as vice-president of operations, to create a network of CARSTAR collision stores across Canada.

"A strong management team is essential for sustained success," says Mercanti, whose privately held company is 82 per cent owned by the Mercanti family and 18 per cent owned by the management and staff at CARSTAR Automotive Canada.

High Common Standards Set

Mercanti says the core strategy was to ensure all of the stores awarded franchises met the same "ethics, standards and consistency that will deliver cost containment, improved turnaround times and customer retention for our insurance partners and CARSTAR stakeholders – that was and is our vision."

That same year, Mercanti began converting existing and acquired franchise operations to make them CARSTAR Automotive Canada locations. The company also began acquiring new locations. It bought two stores in Winnipeg, one in Calgary, one in Montreal and three in the Greater Toronto Area.

That brought the number of locations to 15. Two years later, in 1997, CARSTAR sites numbered 50 and annual sales more than doubled to $25-million.

The company currently earns annual revenue of nearly $100-million and has 91 locations across Canada and 14 insurance contracts with insurers Aviva, Dominion of Canada, RBC General Insurance, Liberty Mutual, Lombard Canada, ING Western Union, Groupe Desjardines Assurances and Certas/The Personal. Suppliers include BASF and Dupont paint companies, Enterprise Rent-A-Car, ADP – IT providers, 3M Canada and NAPA Auto Parts.

Insurance Companies Partners

"The insurance companies are really our insurance partners – we work closely together," notes Mercanti, who has succeeded in earning a growing share of the auto body repairs market. "Our goal is to have $300-million in annual sales and 200 locations across Canada over the next few years."

"Shorter-term goals," he adds, "are to invest more than $1-million on information to connect all our stores by a single computer network and to improve our connectivity to insurance partners and brokers. We're also bringing in a pension/retirement plan for our employees and improving our recruitment of talented technical and management people."

For a potential franchisee the benefits are many, including advertising and promotional exposure and the cache that comes with a national brand.

Automatic Referrals

But the big benefit is the company's sterling reputation, which virtually guarantees business.

"Once we approve a franchisee, the insurance

companies will automatically refer accident claims taking place in that area to that franchisee," Mercanti explains, "because the insurance companies tend to refer their clients to the nearest CARSTAR location."

The faith insurers have in CARSTAR is the result of many years of exemplary service and dedication delivered by Mercanti, who has still further increased the trust factor by using digital camera technology in the collision centres to provide computer-driven video imaging, allowing insurance appraisers to get a good look at vehicle damage without have to take the time to leave their office.

Repairs Faster, Better

The result: Repairs are authorized and completed faster, with better quality than the average body shop – and with less inconvenience to consumers.

"Based on our reputation for honesty and integrity, insurance companies will automatically approve our repair claims in most instances without involving an appraiser," notes Mercanti. "And that saves everyone time and money."

"We're a customer focused business," he continues, "and that includes national guarantees – recognized at CARSTAR stores across Canada and lifetime warrantees on our work. We want to do more than just satisfy the customer – we want to go the extra mile and delight them."

It's all part of an accelerated evolution that Mercanti envisions for CARSTAR and the industry.

"We're trying to elevate the body shop industry to higher standards," adds Mercanti, whose company is highly ranked by the Coyote Vision Group, which represents the North American industry.

Mercanti is marketing his business system to the franchisees with customer satisfaction at the heart of a strategy to make CARSTAR as just familiar to average consumers as Speedy mufflers and Harvey's hamburgers.

"Our objective is to establish a brand presence in Canada," Mercanti explains. "Right now, there's no nationally recognized collision centre brand presence. We want to change that, so if you get in an accident and your insurance company asks you where you want to have your vehicle repaired, CARSTAR comes to mind right away."

Growing Market Share

That key objective is becoming a reality: When CARSTAR Automotive Canada was founded in 1995, it had 0.5 per cent of the Canadian collision repairs market. By the end of 2000 market share had risen to 4.2 per cent. By 2003 it had surpassed 5 per cent – and had reached levels as high as 18 per cent in Hamilton-Niagara and 14.7 per cent in the Greater Toronto Area where locations are most heavily concentrated. Total national market share is expected to reach 6.5 per cent by 2006.

Brand awareness has also been rising steadily from zero in 1995 to an estimated 10.1 per cent by 2003, meaning one person in ten is likely to name CARSTAR as the company name that comes to mind when asked about their preferred repair location following an accident.

While remaining sharply focused on the future, Mercanti takes a moment to reflect on values and life lessons that have taken him to this point.

"My parents have been a huge influence in teaching me values," Mercanti acknowledges. "They're very humble people but also very proud and willing to do so much for their children. Family means a lot. My parents came here with no money, not even knowing how to speak the language. But they had family: They had nothing and they had everything. They gave me great values that have stayed with me my whole life."

Mercanti says success is never achieved alone or in isolation. It's owed to relationships with others.

It's All About People

"When you get right down to it, success in life is really all about people, and building relationships. My wife Roma, our children, our family – that's the focus of my own life, why I do what I do," asserts Mercanti who treasures family time. The long-time YMCA member is also an ardent Handball player.

"I learned from my parents to treat others as I would want to be treated to approach everything with ethics and honesty, to earn the trust of others. For our customers, it's all about efficient, quality work at a reasonable cost, based on trust and dependable performance. Walking your talk – that's so important.

Mercanti intends to continue this approach to life and achieving lasting success.

"We're building our success one relationship at a time. And we owe our success to our management, our stakeholders, our franchisees, our insurance partners, our customers and this incredible country."

Sam Mercanti's tips for success:

1. Adopt strong values and ethics and live up to the high standards you set for yourself.

2. Establish and nurture relationships with other people. People helping each other is the key to achieving success. Treat others as your would like to be treated.

3. Don't die with your dreams still in your heart – make your dreams a reality.

4. Try to be all that you can be. It means hard work but the results are well worth it.

5. Don't deny yourself the simple pleasures of family life and quality time with loved ones.

6. Take calculated risks to achieve success. There is no reward without risk.

7. Go out and achieve – give life your best shot.

8. Internalize a belief system that has confidence in your ability to conceive, believe and achieve.

9. Don't just satisfy your customers. Delight them by going the extra mile and delivering added value.

10. Believe in yourself. We are all capable of doing whatever we put our minds to.

11. Adapt, nurture and grow each day in Mind, Body and Spirit.

Ken Lindsay

Chapter 6

Ken Lindsay

Home Ownership Help
at Mortgage Financial

"It comes down to the volume of business we do. It's buying power. We can benefit the customer, whether they're rich or poor by shopping the market on their behalf to get the best mortgage possible for them at the best terms and rates."

- Ken Lindsay

At a Glance: Ken Lindsay and Mortgage Financial:

Ken Lindsay
Age: 40
Title: President, Mortgage Financial Corporation.
Claim to fame: Lindsay heads highly successful mortgage broker firm and shops the market to find the best possible mortgages for clients. He puts together mortgages that best meet a client's needs. His firm has grown steadily over the years and now provides employment for several brokers plus support staff. It's now one of the largest independent mortgage brokers in south-western Ontario.
Financial Data: Largely undisclosed. However, this is a multi-million-dollar company, growing at an average rate of 30 per cent growth per year.
Personal: Resides in Ancaster with wife Monika. The couple have 3 sons: Max, 9, and five-year-old twins Brad and Jeff.
For More information:
Contact: Mortgage Financial Corporation: (905) 529-2521. Toll Free Line: 1-866-604-8860. Fax: (905) 525-9701.
Address: 12 Ray Street South, Hamilton, Ontario. L8P 3V2.

Chapter 6

Ken Lindsay

Home Ownership Help
at Mortgage Financial

For too many people, the dream of home ownership remains nothing more than a dream.

Ken Lindsay makes that dream a reality.

Lindsay, 40, is a mortgage broker: He shops the market for the best mortgage deals he can find his clients – even those with financial and credit rating issues.

"We take pride in generating savings to the customer," notes Lindsay, president of Mortgage Financial Corporation.

"Whether the client is financially successful or is currently facing financial issues, we can save them some money by shopping the mortgage market to find a deal that best meets their needs," he explains in an interview at company headquarters on Ray Street South, Hamilton.

"There aren't too many people who can go to a bank on their own and get a better deal than we can, generally," Lindsay asserts.

Buying power

"That's because we're also able to exercise a fair amount of buying power, some real financial clout, given the amount of business we bring to the banks," adds Lindsay, very much a hands-on broker who continues to personally arrange mortgages on behalf of his many clients.

"And for those customers who have been turned down by a bank, we're often able to get them a mortgage – sometimes from the same bank that turned them down – by negotiating a deal that works for everyone."

Financial lenders, including banks and trust companies, pay the firm a finder's fee/commission for bringing them ready-to-go mortgage deals involving financially secure borrowers.

A win-win situation

The arrangement also works well for banks, which rely on the broker to bring them mortgage business.

As well, the bank gets to sit back while the

broker does the bulk of the work.

And the bank will withhold any commission until the successful completion of a mortgage deal.

"It's basically a risk-free undertaking for the banks – it's really good for all of the financial institutions," Lindsay notes, "and the banks remain suppliers of the mortgage funds in most cases."

And for would-be homeowners who have credit difficulties and have been turned down by the banks, there is still hope.

Mortgage help for everyone

Mortgage Financial charges a fee to these less-secure clients to arrange a mortgage on their behalf, normally at somewhat higher interest rates to reflect the added degree of risk involved.

"Usually we can negotiate a deal at virtually no cost to the mortgage-borrower – they literally have nothing to lose and everything to gain with lower rates and better terms," Lindsay says.

He notes these clients account for about 75 per cent of his business, "and we can sometimes even beat the rates the banks offer their own staff."

"Even for the clients who are not financially secure, we can often put together a deal that's not a whole lot more expensive than what someone in a more financially advantageous position would be taking on," Lindsay adds.

"It comes down to the volume of business we do – it's buying power," the amiable broker explains.

Even a modest difference in interest rates can prove substantial.

For example, before factoring in property taxes, a $100,000 mortgage, amortized over 20 years (the full lifespan of the mortgage) at a 3 per cent interest rate would cost the borrower $554 in monthly principal-and-interest payments.

The same mortgage with a 4 percent interest rate would push the monthly payments to more than $600. And at 5 per cent, the monthly payment needed increases to $660.

Small rate change: big difference

A further increase of less than one per cent – to 5.75 per cent – inflates the monthly payments to a still more costly $700.

Quite clearly, even a small difference in mortgage interest rates can have a very significant impact on payment levels and affordability.

Lindsay and his Mortgage Financial broker-agents routinely save their clients many thousands of dollars in mortgage payments annually by arranging lower-rate mortgages.

"We can benefit the customer, whether they're well-off or have financial concerns by shopping the market on their behalf to get the best mortgage possible for them at the best terms and rates," Lindsay asserts.

"If they're financially well-off, we can get them better rates and better terms than they'll likely be able to get on their own," he states.

"And, if the client is struggling a little or working through some financial issues, we can, in most cases, get them a pretty good mortgage when they otherwise might not be able to get any mortgage at all," he adds.

Lindsay's Mortgage Financial firm is today one of the largest independent mortgage brokers in south-western Ontario, with business volume in the tens of millions of dollars.

Success story built on determination

How he rose to become a leading mortgage broker and highly successful businessman is a story that begins in the city of Brantford.

Sometimes called the Telephone City, Brantford is famous as the home of Alexander Graham Bell, the late, great inventor of the world's most-used communications device.

Brantford is also renowned as the birthplace of Wayne Gretzky, arguably the greatest hockey player who has ever lived.

The city, which is also the birthplace of the late, great comic actor Phil Hartman, has a leafy charm that extends well beyond the banks of Grand River that runs through it.

But Brantford is also well known for hard times and failed industries. Numerous industries have vacated the city and others have simply closed. In the midst of economic devastation, too many local citizens adopted a "no you can't" attitude toward success.

Yet, it was in this oft-times negative civic atmosphere and outlook that a young Ken Lindsay's entrepreneurial spirit would emerge.

Driven by desire to Achieve

"I think I've always wanted to succeed in a business of some kind," Lindsay recalls.

Driven by a desire to achieve, Lindsay left Brantford for Hamilton in 1982 where he attended McMaster University and completed a Bachelor of Economics (B.Econ) degree in 1986.

After graduating, he began working as a salesman in Toronto for the 3M company, selling business equipment, including fax machines to corporate customers.

"Fax machines were brand new to the market back then," he recalls with a smile, "and I can remember having to convince many CEOs to fax instead of courier information to their clients."

But convince them he did, rising quickly to become one the company's most successful salesmen in Ontario.

He was also earning $47,000 a year at a time when $30,000 was considered a substantial middle-class income.

Discovering the value of real estate

During his first year out of university, Lindsay invested some of his 3M salesman earnings into the purchase both halves of a two-family, semi-detached duplex house in Hamilton's leafy Westdale community – the home of McMaster University – which he then rented out as student housing.

The experience of buying up real estate provided Lindsay with some personal experience of what it means to obtain and maintain mortgages.

It also taught him location and timing are everything.

"Not only had I bought two houses ideally

located right near the university, I also bought just before the real estate boom," he recalls, noting he bought the duplex for $110,000 in 1987 and sold just two years later for $220,000 – twice what he'd originally paid.

Huge return on investment

The huge return on investment would later be used, in part, to buy his own home and as seed money to fund the start-up of his own company.

The income from the student rental housing also boosted his already substantial income from 3M, a sales job that pushed Lindsay to find the most effective marketing methods around to sell relatively unknown fax machine products.

"It was an opportunity – and a challenge," he recalls with a grin.

"Fax machines were a new concept and they were expensive," he adds.

"The cheapest model was $6,000 – and the actual machine was no bigger than the ones out today, but it came in a big case to help justify the price."

A fateful foray into mortgage brokering

After three years with 3M, Lindsay was ready to take on another challenging opportunity.

He found that opportunity in Oakville – and it marked his first, fateful foray into the world of mortgage brokering.

In 1989, he began working as a mortgage broker for Goldmore Financial (now known as The

Mortgage Department), an Oakville-based mortgage broker.

That same year, he decided to set down some roots, and he bought a house in Burlington.

Lindsay soon discovered that although he was working for a mortgage broker in Oakville, "most of my clients were in Hamilton, so I was also being drawn to this city."

"I really like Hamilton," Lindsay asserts.

"It's smaller than Toronto but it still has everything a big city has to offer, and the people are very friendly," he notes.

"I also found the lenders here in Hamilton to be quite approachable. This is a blue-collar town but approaching the size of a metropolis."

Lindsay decided to lay down more Steel City roots, actively seeking out local lenders while also building the bulk of his clientele base in Hamilton.

Winning combination in Hamilton

"I found the winning combination in Hamilton," he explains.

"Hamilton offers a good source of approachable private lenders and a sizeable client base of people who need mortgages and don't hesitate to turn to us for service and advice."

The transition from broker to broker-owner took place incrementally, over the course of a few years, during which time Lindsay built a solid reputation as a straight-forward broker who worked closely with clients to achieve the best mortgages possible on their behalf.

His growing success was also forged on his willingness to listen closely to what clients were saying concerning both their need for a mortgage and their income and affordability concerns. His approach inevitably resulted in the creation of custom-made mortgages and very satisfied clients.

And his approach succeeded in attracting a seemingly never-ending series of referrals that continues to this day.

In fact, his company owes much of its strong, continued prosperity to referrals based on exemplary past performance.

The dawn of Mortgage Financial

In 1991, Lindsay took the plunge and founded his own company on King Street West in Hamilton, near Queen Street.

And starting up Mortgage Financial in Canada's Steel City was not without risk.

"It's always a major adjustment to go from something that's relatively secure to something that's new and different," Lindsay recalls.

"But I knew this was something I wanted to do, something I really had to do and I was prepared to take on the risks of venturing out on my own."

Although Toronto was then, as now, the main financial centre of Ontario and Canada, Lindsay saw in Hamilton, a vibrant city rich in potential.

"With Hamilton, I saw a service-oriented opportunity," he recalls, "and I got into this business when it was relatively young so I could build on my modest investment in my company."

"In Canada, brokers are involved in only about 22 per cent of all mortgages, while in the United States, the level is 78 per cent – so there's a lot of growth potential for the mortgage brokering business in this country," he adds.

"Back in 1991, my company was very small," he recalls. "It was just myself and one other broker – but we were ready to grow from there."

Lindsay would come to outgrow that first location and he moved, in 1998, to his current head-quarters on Ray Street, just a few blocks away from the original offices.

He owns the stately office building on Ray Street South – purchased for $171,000 – that was converted from a 130-year-old mansion a short walk from the Scottish Rite.

Risk level increased to spur growth

"That year, 1998, was really a very tough year," Lindsay recalls, shaking his head.

"I owed $50,000 in taxes at that point, plus I had just put $50,000 down on the Ray Street building and had a mortgage for the rest," he adds.

"My wife had just had twins and we bought a van. Altogether, it was a larger debt-load than I'd ever experienced and I had to work many long, hard hours to generate sufficient income to keep it all under control."

Weathering that financial situation gave the young mortgage broker some first-hand sympathy for what many people encounter when they take on the heady costs associated with a mortgage, other debts and, of course, the never-ending costs of raising a family.

Simply put, Lindsay also came to appreciate, in 1998, what it means to be stretched to max.

"That was the most risk I've ever taken on in my life," he acknowledges with raised eyebrows.

"But it motivated me to succeed," he adds.

"I know what our clients go through. I've been there. I know what it's like to wonder if you'll qualify for a mortgage and what it's like to have to make those payments."

The experience would also have a profound affect on Lindsay.

"To stay on top of it all, I consolidated all my debts into a better package and started working away at paying it down," he explains.

"But it was necessary at that time to take on this debt and the business had to rank high on the priority list. It had to be done – so I did it."

Pay-as-you-go approach

"I now pay as I go, all the time, as much as humanly possible," Lindsay asserts.

"And I try to take on very little debt. In fact, I make a real effort to keep my fixed costs and debt to a minimum."

There's also no question his own experience with grappling with personal mortgages and debt helped make Lindsay a better, more effective and understanding mortgage broker.

Inside his expansive Ray Street building with ornate woodwork and high-ceilings, Lindsay can often be found on the phone or plying the computer at his oft-cluttered desk (yet he can somehow manage to find any desired document on that desk).

In running Mortgage Financial, he's assisted by his brother Mike Lindsay and a dedicated support staff. Also helping drive Mortgage Financial to new heights is a team of broker-agents.

Team effort

"I really like our office atmosphere," Lindsay acknowledges with a grin.

"They're a great group and we enjoy bouncing ideas off each other. It's impressive when I think that we have a large group of people all helping each other out."

While he still handles some deals directly, Lindsay is also heavily involved in running his office, handling payroll and provide problem-solving and direction skills to the company.

"To a certain extent, I depend on my broker-agents to build business volume," he explains.

"But I also still enjoy arranging mortgages myself whenever the opportunity presents itself," Lindsay adds.

"Having the Kronas Group – one of the largest private lenders in the Hamilton area – right in our building is also a big benefit," he notes.

"Getting financing for a mortgage is often as simple as going upstairs in this building for a visit with someone from the Kronas Group."

Soon after Mortgage Financial's founding in 1991, the young company began achieving some impressive profit growth.

That trend has carried on, and the company's

profits have continued to average 30 per cent growth over the past few years.

The company now arranges more than $100-million worth of mortgages annually and grosses in excess of $2-million in annual revenue.

Much of the fast growing profit – more precise figures are confidential – is reinvested in the company and in the financing of mortgages.

Impressive growth

"Our profit growth has really exceeded all expectations," Lindsay smiles, noting Mortgage Financial is now one of the largest independent mortgage broker firms in the whole of south-western Ontario.

The company has 28 broker-agents and support staff in Hamilton, plus another three broker-agents at a branch office in Brantford.

The year 1991 also marked another very important milestone: The same year Lindsay started up his company, he also married his girlfriend Monika.

His wife, also now 40, bought their family home in 1990 for $130,000 and the happy couple took residence there on marrying the following year.

They rented in out a basement apartment for the next six years until the house was sold in 1997 for $165,000. His wife is also no slouch on the business front – she's a full partner in the highly successful Fast Eddies drive-through fast food chain of restaurants.

The couple now reside with their three children: Max 9, and five-year-old twins Brad and Jeff, in the Meadowlands neighbourhood in Hamilton's Ancaster community.

Lindsay believes much of his firm's success is owed to its prominence in the Hamilton market and its ability to arrange an array of mortgages.

"Our business volume helps us achieve successful placement of mortgages at more than competitive rates," he notes, "and I think that, more than anything else, has helped us to grow, year by year. I anticipate growth continuing in the 30 per cent range, but I'd be happy with even half of that."

And Lindsay still clearly enjoys his hands-on approach to brokering mortgages.

"We do all the negotiating and shopping around for rates on the client's behalf," he says, adding "in most cases, most of shopping is done in my head because I know which lenders to use and where to place a given mortgage."

The shopping is also done in advance of meeting with clients. By the time an actual meeting between customer and broker takes place, the Mortgage Financial representative usually has in place a short list of advantageous mortgage options for the client to choose from.

Clients also benefit from Lindsay's access to a large pool of lenders, the negotiating clout his volume of business gives him with the banks and his industry savvy and his ability to negotiate a win-win deal for the customer and lender.

Tailor-made mortgages

"We can custom tailor a mortgage to the customer's needs right off the bat because we have so many lenders and mortgage products to choose from," he notes.

To tailor a mortgage to the client's needs, Lindsay or one of his broker-agents will sit down with the customer and determine what their income levels are, how much mortgage they can afford to carry, what payment schedules are best-suited for them, how determined they are to pay off the mortgage and what other options are worth considering.

For example, mortgage options can include the length of amortization – whether the total mortgage life span runs 10, 15, 20 or 25 years.

A shorter amortization means the mortgage is paid off entirely much more quickly, but the weekly or monthly payments are much higher than they would be with a longer amortization period.

Regardless of the amortization, weekly payments (or payments every two weeks) are often recommended as they effectively translate into an extra monthly payment each year, which in turn means the mortgage is being reduced a little more quickly and conveniently.

Many mortgage options to choose from

Mortgage options can include a number of variations in the length of the term – whether one wants to go six months, one year, two years, three years or five years before renewing the mortgage.

The borrower may also want to knock down the size of the mortgage by having extra payment privileges that allow for larger payments or a lump sum payment or both during the mortgage term.

A down payment of 25 per cent or more of the purchase price will not only dramatically reduce the size of the resulting mortgage, it will also save the borrower costs of getting the mortgage insured by Canada Mortgage and Housing Corporation. CMHC insurance – for high leverage loans of more than 75 per cent of the purchase price – often adds several thousand dollars to the size of the mortgage.

There are still also mortgage variations, including fixed rates that lock you in at a set interest rate for the mortgage term, and variable rates, which are tied to market interest rates and follow those rates up or down.

Variable rates are often considered attractive to borrowers if they anticipate rates remaining low or falling. But if rates rise, the borrower pays the higher rate.

Fixed rates are sometimes a little more costly, but they provide the stability of certainty over the level of interest rate the borrower will pay.

Lindsay notes his ability to draw on a number of lenders means he can offer just about any mortgage package combination imaginable.

"If you, as an individual, are still limiting yourself to one lending institution, you pretty much have to take what you can get – and that's often not the greatest deal that's out there in the marketplace," he observes.

Sense of satisfaction

Lindsay also derives a considerable sense of satisfaction in helping clients obtain the mortgage that's best for them.

"It's a great feeling when we're able to get someone a terrific interest rate and terms," he says.

"And it's also a great feeling when someone who figured they'd never be able to buy a house is able to get a mortgage through us and achieve the dream of home ownership," he adds.

Despite the obvious merit of using a broker's services, the mortgage broker industry hasn't always had a sterling reputation.

As recently as the early 1970s, brokers were viewed with a disdain normally reserved for used car salesmen.

That image, never wholly accurate, was seriously outdated, going back to an era in which there was little regulation of the mortgage broker industry and greater potential for abuse.

The industry is today governed by the Ontario Ministry of Consumer and Financial Services and there are clear-cut rules and regulations for fair conduct.

Unfortunately, old, tired and largely unfair impressions can sometimes linger on.

Until recent decades, mortgage brokers were seen as lenders of last resort, unsavoury people who arranged loans, at punitive interest rates, for equally unsavoury clients or for hapless victims who couldn't afford to take on any mortgage or loan.

Such victims then found high-interest mortgages to be crushing debt loads.

Improving image

That unseemly image of the mortgage broker was rarely deserved and largely inaccurate, except for the enduring role as a lender of last resort: Mortgage brokers have, in fact, traditionally been just that:

lenders of last resort, the last people you can turn to when the financial institutions have turned you down.

And that role – a heroic role in the eyes of many borrowers – has continued to some degree right up to the present.

Heroic role continues

"A good 25 per cent of our business comes from people who have been turned down by their bank for a mortgage," Lindsay notes, "with the other 75 per cent consists mainly of people who have no difficulty getting a mortgage – they just want to use our broker services so we can shop the market to get them better rates."

"But it was the reverse when I started," he adds. "The vast majority of people using broker services back then had been turned down by the banks and were using us as a lender of last resort. And that was only ten years ago."

Despite the trend to lower-risk lending, Lindsay makes it clear he'd "never want to give up that 25 per cent of higher risk lending, because it's a good source of business and a great way to help people out."

"In fact, we sometimes have higher-risk borrowers coming directly to us, without even going to a bank first, because they don't feel comfortable dealing with a bank and they fear being rejected for a mortgage," he elaborates.

"We're happy to deal with low-risk and high-risk borrowers."

And in today's uncertain times, there are growing numbers of people facing severe financial difficulties for the first time, he points out.

"Not only is the old life-long jobs era long over, we've seen a lot of corporate downsizing and elimination of jobs," Lindsay notes.

"Today, more people than not have credit problems, and we do what we can to help," he adds.

Turning to mortgage brokers for help

"We'll even help people get credit cards and re-establish their credit ratings and, of course, get them a good mortgage," Lindsay explains.

"We're in the business of giving a lot of people an opportunity they didn't think even existed – and they're not in any way overpaying for that opportunity."

Lindsay notes greater numbers of people are turning to mortgage brokers – and he expects that trend to continue.

"More and more people are gradually coming around to the idea of using a mortgage broker to do all the work for you – for free in most cases – to arrange your mortgage," he observes.

Brokering better deals

"After all, people think nothing of using an insurance broker to get the best insurance deal, and it's becoming that way with using mortgage brokers to get the best mortgage deals," he adds.

In fact, it's difficult to understand why anyone would not want to use the services of a reputable mortgage broker.

"We'll often do 100-plus mortgages a month, whereas most people will do perhaps one or two in their lifetime – so how can they compete with us for the best deal? We know which lenders to go to which deals can be improved, all of the ins and outs of mortgages – it's what we do."

And the benefits of using a broker go beyond the financial. "We'll get you the same or lower rate than the bank is offering – usually a lower rate," Lindsay asserts. "And we'll get the job done more quickly and efficiently with less aggravation for the borrower to deal with," he notes.

"We can also provide substantially more choice in mortgage products and terms," he adds.

"More people are finding they'd much rather leave the task of arranging a mortgage to an expert, a mortgage broker, who can do all the work for them to get the deal that's best for them."

Ken Lindsay's tips for success:

1. Use debt as a tool to achieve the wealth that equity brings. Recognize that debt to gain an appreciating asset – such as a mortgage to buy a house – is good debt that can leave you further ahead long-term.

2. Build equity as this means building wealth. Why pay rent to a landlord when you can take on a mortgage and ownership of your own home – and your own destiny.

3. Consider renting out part of your home so that your tenants pay your mortgage for you.

4. Control debt – don't let debt control you. Even good debt can be too much of a good thing. It's important to reduce debts.

5. Think about what you want to achieve and set about making your dreams a reality.

6. If you'd like to start a business, first get experience and education in that field.

7. Do market research. Take a methodical, thorough approach to building the business.

8. Be prepared to work long and hard to earn a measure of success in your endeavour.

9. Don't be afraid to take on debt – and risk – to finance the achievement of your dreams.

10. Any risk you take on should be a calculated risk. You should be confident of success.

Artist's illustration of The Palace, a Reimer Construction project to be built on the South Service Road in Burlington, just south of the QEW.

Winning Ways Vol. 2
Special Section
Celebrating Success
Reimer Country

A Remarkable Burlington Family Discusses
Their Successful Past and Promising Future

Rudy Reimer Sr. (seated) with Randy Heine,
Rudy K. Reimer and Teresa Reimer

Rudy Reimer with former U.S. President George Bush

Chapter 7

Rudy Reimer Sr.

A Multi-faceted Success Story

"It fills us with satisfaction to consistently exceed our customers' expectations."

- Rudy Reimer.

At a Glance: Rudy Reimer Sr.
and Reimer Construction:

Rudy Reimer
Age: 66
Title: President & CEO, Reimer Construction Limited.
Awards: Reimer is a proud recipient of the highly prestigious *Queen's Golden Jubilee Medal*, honouring his "significant contribution" to Canada and his fellow Canadians. Canada's Governor General has presented him with the *Commemorative Medal For The 125th Anniversary Of The Confederation Of Canada*, to recognize his "significant contribution to compatriots, community and to Canada." You can also find him listed in the influential *Who's Who National Registry* under executives and professionals of note. And he's been honoured with the coveted *Lifetime Achievement Award* from the Burlington Chamber of Commerce and he's won many other awards – too many to list.
Claim to fame: Major developer of commercial and residential projects. Commercial project's tenants read like a Who's Who of Canadian business leaders. He's transformed Burlington's skyline and is turning the city into a major commercial centre.
Financial Data: Undisclosed. Successful Private firm.
Personal: Resides in Burlington with wife Teresa Reimer. Father of Rudy K. Reimer and Darlene Heine.
For More information:
Contact: Reimer Construction: (905) 336-8775
Fax: (905) 336-7936.
Address: 9th Floor, Reimer Millennium Tower, 5500 North Service Road, Burlington, Ontario, L7L 6W6.

Chapter 7

Rudy Reimer Sr.
A Multi-faceted Success Story

Rudy Reimer continues to build a truly successful life others can only dream of. But his impressive business growth is only one aspect of a multi-faceted success story that includes much more than great wealth and achievement.

Indeed, the most obvious evidence of Reimer's success is found in the dynamic developer's numerous office complexes lining the highway from Burlington to Oakville. After escaping war-torn Germany, Reimer literally went from rags to riches in Burlington, and so transformed the local landscape that it's been dubbed 'Reimer Country'.

Yet, Reimer's greatest source of pride lies not in his huge projects or considerable wealth but in the enduring favourable impact he's had on his family, his customers and all those whose lives have been touched by this highly accomplished developer. Simply put, he enjoys making a profound, positive difference in other peoples' lives.

A visit to the impressive glass towers dotting the Burlington landscape provides an indication of the importance Reimer, president and CEO of Reimer Construction Limited, places on his family. Reimer's sense of pride and the admiration he holds for his loved ones is always very much in evidence.

Proud Patriarch

Reimer is the proud patriarch of a family of achievers, including wife Teresa, head of T. Reimer Design Consultants Inc.; son Rudy, president of R. K. Reimer Developments; daughter Darlene, an ardent community supporter; and son-in-law Randy Heine, president of Crystal Ridge Development Services. "My son Rudy serves as the engineer, architect and superintendent of our projects," Reimer smiles proudly, explaining that while his son lacks official engineering and architectural credentials the quality of his work is such that it normally needs no more than a brief standards check by accredited professionals. All buildings are within building codes while featuring original designs that allow maximum views through sun shielding reflective glass; and healthy air circulation.

One way Reimer keeps his customers happy is by adding value to his work while minimizing costs: Instead of spending $200,000 on architectural fees from the concept stage on, Reimer initially envisions the building, then personally creates a rough sketch. That sketch is then turned over to son Rudy for elaboration and added details. Only after that point are the plans turned over to an architect for finalizing formal blueprints. Costs are also saved by having his son Rudy

K. Reimer do his own negotiating with trades people rather than hire a negotiator.

The result of cost-cutting, quality-enhancing efforts is to provide premium, luxury office space to tenants at a bargain rate: Often a highly competitive $25-per-square-foot of gross rent.

"We stay within practical limitations of what our customers can afford to give the customer the most value at a fairly low rate," Reimer explains. "We say that for $25 per square foot, you won't find better value than what we're offering."

Healthy Buildings

"It's so important for employee comfort and tenant comfort to give people a sense of space and the ability to see outside without being too hot in the summer or cold in the winter," Reimer explains, in an interview at his office decorated with family portraits. "We don't have any sick building syndrome, because we continually pump fresh air into our buildings and release stale air. We maintain a constant, moderate fresh air level."

The blue-glassed building exteriors and building systems are clearly impressive. But also impressive are the buildings' elegant interiors. The office space varies in themes and influences, but all exude a warm, understated opulence. Here again, Reimer smiles with pride.

"**Teresa** does our very excellent interior design work," he says of his wife. "She works with tenants and the presidents of large corporations and they love to work with her, as she has practical, suitable ideas that give them the look and image they need. It's good for the companies and their employees – it means high credibility for the companies."

Reimer notes Teresa treats each business separately to come up with an interior design best suited to that **particular firm**. Teresa Reimer adds value to building interiors through her design work. Many building interiors are of marble and expensive woods. Plants, trees, flowers and warm decorative touches are everywhere.

He's also proud of his wife's exhaustive work with the **Junior League** of Hamilton-Burlington Inc., which has performed a great deal of charitable work and helped many worthy causes achieve their goals.

"Teresa's goal is to satisfy the customer and the community – and that's our common goal too at Reimer Construction and the other companies – it's a goal we all share," Reimer says.

"It fills us with satisfaction to exceed our customers' expectations."

Daughter Darlene Helped

Reimer also speaks with considerable pride and affection of his daughter Darlene. "She helped us out in our restaurant business years ago, and made a real difference. Then she decided to devote her time to raising her family and I certainly respect and support that decision – that's an important job and she's good at whatever she puts her mind to."

"My whole life is dedicated to my family," concurs Darlene, 40, who became Darlene Heine when at age 20, she married Randy Heine, the president of

Crystal Ridge Development Services, a company that performs much of the post-construction painting and service work associated with Reimer projects.

"And I like to work behind the scenes on behalf of the community and my family," adds Darlene. "I always strive to a good role model, an honest, hard-working citizen."

Darlene recalls her involvement in the family business starting when she was just 12 years old. "I did some filing work and watered the office plants – that was a long time ago," she chuckles.

A few years later, her involvement in the company took on a managerial bent when she began accounting and operations work for three restaurants that were located in her father's buildings on the South Service Road in Burlington.

Darlene Takes Pride In Work

"We provided breakfasts and lunches and also banquets on weekends – it was a service my dad was providing for the tenants," she explains. "My dad's always been very service-oriented and I took a lot of pride in providing the best restaurant services possible to his tenants."

Darlene stayed with the restaurants business for several years until she married husband and best friend Randy Heine, now 44, who also hails from a construction family and often jokes that "we were born with a shovel in our hand." Randy's been active many years in coaching youth sports, achieving 3M's Coach of the Year Award. Randy also enjoys competing in marathons.

Married at age 20, Darlene gave birth a year later to Darryl, the first of two children, both sons, and it was then that her focus shifted heavily to family life.

"I'm a mother and caregiver, and decided to become a full-time homemaker and focus on the children and their activities," she explains, noting the Darryl, now 19, is interested in a career in fire-fighting, attending college in Toronto, while playing Varsity Hockey for the Seneca Sting. Ryan, 16, like his brother, is an accomplished athlete excelling in rugby playing for Team Ontario. He recently won Silver at the Canadian Nationals.

"My other passion is volunteer work," adds Darlene who was an avid volunteer for every sports organization her boys were involved with. "If everyone does just a little part, it's amazing what we can accomplish together." Darlene also enjoys her time spent as a Joseph Brant Memorial Hospital auxiliary volunteer. She's also worked with the Mental Health Program through the Acts of Kindness program.

Dad A Big Influence

Darlene says her father was a major influence who is partly responsible for the sense of drive that has made her a low-key success on the home front and in the community.

"My dad taught us the work ethic and that we should work hard to achieve our dreams. I think that's always stayed with me… my dad builds a great product and he's an excellent businessman "

Darlene Heine and the other Reimer family members aren't the only ones praising the developer.

Reimer has frequently been lauded for his support of Joseph Brant Memorial Hospital and the JBMH Foundation: "Your sponsorship will allow us to stay on the leading edge of medical technology and help countless patients... the ultimate beneficiaries of your generosity," states a February 2003 letter of praise from Ebbe Marquardsen, JBMH vice-president of development and community relations.

"Your support is essential to maintaining the high quality of health care that you have come to expect at Joseph Brant Memorial Hospital," concludes Marquardsen, on thanking Reimer for a $10,000 gift in support of the hospital's New Tools For Life campaign through JBMH's Annual Crystal Ball celebration. The donation was merely the most recent in a long string of donations Reimer has provided the hospital.

Reimer says he enjoys "helping people who are less fortunate," and recognizes "how important it is to have a good hospital in our community – the more we do for our hospitals, the more we do for ourselves as a community."

Many Worthy Causes Helped

And that's just a small sample of Reimer's generosity. He's helped an array of worthy causes over the years, including the Chedoke-McMaster Children's Hospital in Hamilton, the Mother's Day Telethon, and Halton Women's Place and at one time served simultaneously on 20 different boards and committees. He can reflect on a remarkable life with success based on honest, ethical conduct and genuine concern and compassion for the community.

Of course Reimer has also left a long-lasting positive impression on business and community leaders and the favourable way he is viewed by others is yet another meaningful measurement of his success.

"My experience with Reimer Construction has been that the company has always conducted themselves in a professional and effective manner," states Matt Koevoets, executive director of public works and environment for the City of Burlington.

Current Burlington Mayor Robert MacIsaac has expressed appreciation for Reimer's tireless efforts at helping the community and his ability to bring major businesses to Burlington. Indeed, Reimer has received more than 20 awards from the City of Burlington celebrating his achievements. And former Burlington Mayor Roly Bird has expressed gratitude for Reimer's work on the Burlington Cultural Centre board of directors; for a decade of involvement in Burlington's Business Development Committee; and for many years of support for worthy causes. Bird expressed further appreciation for a "positive working relationship."

Respect of World Leaders

Reimer hasn't just made a favourable impression on municipal politicians. His business insight and thoughtful reflections on world events are also appreciated by world leaders. He's met and conversed with former U.S. presidents George H. Bush and Bill Clinton; Queen Elizabeth and the Queen Mum; Prime Minister Jean Chretien; incoming Prime Minister Paul Martin and former prime ministers Joe Clark and Brian Mulroney; former Ontario premiers Mike Harris and Ernie Eves; and former British Prime Minister

Margaret Thatcher. Indeed, a personal message from former U.S. President Bill Clinton thanks Reimer for his input and assures the developer "I am doing everything I can to help us meet the crucial challenges that face all of us."

Reimer also accepted an invitation to become a member of the Executive Advisory Board of the highly prestigious Gorbachev Foundation/Canada, established by former Soviet Union leader Mikhail Gorbachev to promote world peace and economic development following the break-up of the USSR.

And Reimer has served on dozens of boards – including the Hamilton Tiger-Cat Corporate Advisory Board – plus committees and organizations where he's rubbed shoulders with leading business executives, medical professionals and prominent politicians.

He's served on the boards and committees of area hospitals and served six years as vice-president and two years as Business Development Committee chairman of the Burlington Chamber of Commerce.

Reimer also served 10 years as chairman of the Toronto Home Builders Halton Region Liaison; seven years as vice-president and honorary chairman of the Burlington Visitor & Convention Bureau; five years as vice-president of the Burlington Cultural Centre; and five years as vice-chairman of the Hamilton Philharmonic Orchestra Board, to name but a few of his many positions over the years. And he's served more than 40 years as president and CEO of Reimer Construction.

Reimer's Help A Blessing

On the religious front, Reimer made a very substantial contribution to ably assist the Crossroads

Family of Ministries with the Crossroads Centre, which is situated in an enormous landmark building on former Reimer lands on North Service Road near Brant Street in Burlington.

As Richard Brown, corporate vice-president of Crossroads, notes: "Rudy, I'm reminded daily of your gracious contribution to the success of the Crossroads Centre each day as I drive to and from work."

A generous contributor to many worthy causes, Reimer also donated funds to erect a huge, white neon cross, on the QEW near Vineland, pointing travellers to God and bearing the message 'Jesus loves you'. Reimer's donation was at the request of Pastor Henry Wiebe, who was formerly Reimer's Sunday school teacher.

Wiebe also thanked Reimer for donating funds to help Vladimir and Anna Bortsov's ministry efforts in Ontario. "A special thanks for your assistance in supporting this family," Wiebe stated in a June 5, 2003, letter. "God bless you for your contribution."

Reimer humbly acknowledges that Wiebe also had a profound impact on his life. "He taught me Christian values that have stayed with me my whole life – I'm glad to help," Reimer explains.

Success Celebrated

Not surprisingly, Reimer's remarkable success and many contributions to society have been the subject of numerous newspaper and magazine articles.

He's also been featured in the book Enterprise 2000 and in the previous volume of Winning Ways, which drew considerable response, including this note of appreciation from Ancaster chiropractor Dr. Omar Pervez: "My appreciation lies from the motivation I gained after reading about your story in the book Winning Ways. Very interesting to me was how you managed to build your construction and commercial empire after escaping war-torn Germany... I enjoyed it immensely, gaining much motivation and ambition from your success... thank you for sharing your story, it was touching and inspiring."

Reimer has also received numerous accolades from business associates, including words of praise from Hans Rudolf Wohrl, owner of major department stores in Germany and an investor in Reimer properties in Burlington. Wohrl lauds Reimer for his "reliable and always fair cooperation."

Gold Medal Performance

Indeed, when it comes to business and serving the community, Reimer's a gold medal performer.

In October 2002, Reimer, 65, was awarded the highly prestigious *Queen's Golden Jubilee Medal* in Royal recognition of his "significant contribution" to Canada and his fellow Canadians.

The same month, the **Governor General** presented him with the *Commemorative Medal For The 125th Anniversary Of The Confederation Of Canada*, lauding his "significant contribution to compatriots, community and to Canada."

Reimer has also been named *Developer Of The year* and he's won an award of merit from the Ontario government.

He's also the first-ever recipient of a *Lifetime*

Achievement Award from the Burlington Chamber of Commerce, honouring his "dedication, vision and passion as a developer."

In addition to his seemingly endless string of accolades, awards and medals, Reimer is listed in the highly influential *Who's Who National Register* under prominent North American executives/professionals.

Reimer Construction was also a finalist for the International Prix Excellence Awards, placing in the top 22 of competing companies from 145 countries.

Although he prefers not to discuss his company's financial affairs in detail, Reimer provides an indication when he notes that in 1989, Reimer Construction paid about $360,000 in property taxes. By 1993 the property tax bill had risen to $1.2-million and it now runs into the millions of dollars.

Indeed, as he surveys the stretching landscape from the glass walls of his penthouse office, Reimer exudes the self-confidence of a savvy dealmaker and developer who has achieved enviable business success.

Reimer's Challenging Life

But how he survived wartime persecution and poverty to rise to his position of power and influence is a truly intriguing and inspiring story. Reimer's life story begins in southern Ukraine, in a small village near the Black Sea, where he was born to a Mennonite family that spoke a Low German dialect, somewhat similar to Dutch.

He was the family's only son in a family that also featured had two daughters: Frida, a teacher, who would later marry a produce cultivator in Beamsville,

Ontario. Marianne would marry a heart specialist and general surgeon in Virginia, USA.

Since Ukraine was then part of the Russia-controlled Soviet Union, at school, Reimer had to learn Russian in order to comprehend classroom instruction.

Crowded Existence

The family lived a crowded existence in a house offering less than 700 square feet of living space – about the size of his current bathroom.

As a religious minority in Ukraine, the Reimer family was subjected to persecution. And it soon got worse: In the early 1940s, with World War II raging, the Russians periodically walked into his relatives' homes and removed one family member or another for questioning. Jail terms often followed. Some relatives were never seen or heard from again.

"Then," Reimer recalls, "when I was about five, the Germans came marching into our German-speaking village in Ukraine. They told us: 'You're Germans – you're coming with us,' and we were evacuated out of Ukraine and taken to Germany."

The final 200 kilometres of their three-week-long journey was on foot across rough terrain.

They would spend the next year living in barracks housing in a refugee camp in Germany.

At age 6, Reimer and family were again on the move just as World War II was grinding to a close and he recalls seeing "many rockets and bullets fly through the air – that was when we had to go to the under-ground shelter for security."

"I can remember walking past Dresden and

through Berlin when these cities were being bombed," he recalls, nearly 60 years later in an interview at office in Burlington. "What I remember most is how the cities lit up when they were bombed, and the glow as they burned," he adds.

Dad Forced To Join Army

Although a peaceful Mennonite, his father, Peter Reimer, was forced to join the German army – the alternative to not enlisting was a bullet through the head – and he was sent to the Russian Front in 1944, just one month before the war ended. At that time, while his father served on the Russian Front, Reimer and his mother and sisters moved into the home of an aunt, who was married to a German army officer.

Then, in the dying months of the war, the Russians captured Peter Reimer. And when they questioned him, he answered first in German, then in Russian. This proved to be a nearly fatal mistake.

It led his captors to accuse him of being a spy. A gun was pointed at his head.

The trigger was pulled. And the bullet shot through his hat, missing his head.

Having cheated death, Peter Reimer was allowed to live – but with a life sentence of hard labour as a Siberian Gulag prisoner.

"Opa," as he was affectionately known by his grandchildren, wore his famous cap with entry and exit bullet hole marks until the end of his life.

"We didn't even know he'd been captured," Reimer recalls.

"We had no knowledge whatsoever of his whereabouts for 10 years – we could only assume he was alive, as my mother had the belief God would bring them safely together again, alive and well."

By this point, Reimer was still a young child. He was left with his mother Anna and sisters Frida, 4, and Marianne, 1, in what would become the partitioned, Soviet-controlled East Berlin area.

Troubles Continued

The war ended, but Reimer family troubles continued. Anna Reimer was questioned by the Russian occupiers and made her husband's mistake of answering in Russian. She was taken for questioning.

Anna Reimer was released temporarily after a prominent relative intervened.

She was told to return to the police station the following morning.

"My mother knew where this was likely to end up," Reimer asserts, "so she decided we would all escape from the Russian sector near the Berlin area."

Anna Reimer and her three children walked in the dark to the train station where the family hid in the bushes.

As the train pulled into the station and slowed down, the mother and her three children crawled quickly between the slowly moving wheels of a boxcar, emerging on the other side where the boxcar doors were located.

"My mother knocked, the door opened, and we were pulled inside," Reimer recollects.

"A moment later, the door was wrenched open and a guard pointed a gun right at us," Reimer adds, his face drawn tight from the vivid memory.

"The guard was very angry and said he didn't

remember us getting on the train and then he demanded a full passenger count – we all had a very sick feeling," he recalls.

"But one of the men in our boxcar told him there would be no counting as everyone was legally on board," he adds.

"The guard then just shrugged his shoulders and walked away."

Once they were safely in what was then West Germany, Reimer excelled in school and skipped several grades during the years the family lived there.

The Promised Land

Then, in 1949, the Reimer family immigrated to Canada – the trip was paid for by church groups as the family had virtually no money – and moved in with an uncle in a small Mennonite community at Camden, on the outskirts of Vineland, Ontario.

"The vision I had of Canada at that time was that all the telephone poles were made of gold," Reimer recalls.

"That was the only disappointment that we have ever received in Canada."

Reimer took quickly to his adopted country, working hard to learn to speak English and eagerly walking six kilometres to school.

He also eagerly grasped opportunities, including a chance to get involved in some summer work as a farm labourer.

"During summers, I had the great privilege of thinning peaches, picking strawberries and other fruits," Reimer recollects, adding the job taught him one thing: "I never want to become a fruit farmer."

"But I consider it to be a privilege and an honour to live in a country with wonderful, endless opportunities," he adds.

A Builder Is Born

By the time he was 18, Reimer had already seized another opportunity: The chance to work on residential construction sites during his summer holidays.

But he thoroughly enjoyed this work and it would later become a source of solid, full-time employment after he left high school.

As he continued working in construction, Reimer became skilful at building footings and would eventually become knowledgeable in all phases of new home construction, including the design and building of kitchen cabinets.

He also studied blue prints and building codes every spare moment he could find.

It wasn't uncommon for Reimer to sit up reading building plans until well after midnight, making himself intimately familiar with every aspect of home construction.

He became an expert in plumbing, electrical, carpentry, tiling and framing applications and would go on to build more than 2,000 homes – roughing-in at least half of them himself, with help from carpenters.

While he was still in his teens, Reimer often astonished developers with his intimate knowledge of all matters in construction.

More than once, the young worker found himself promoted to foreman after nonchalantly solving a complicated building problem – saving the developer a good deal of money in the process.

"To get ahead in life, sometimes you have to do a little homework," Reimer explains.

"My hobby was learning everything I possibly could about construction – and that's still my hobby," he adds.

"For me, business and serving the community is my greatest hobby and my greatest challenge."

Going It Alone

Reimer was forging impressive success in business – and he then decided to go into business for himself.

Starting up a construction firm was for Reimer an easy decision: He thoroughly enjoyed working on homes.

"In 1954, I worked a year for a contractor in the Vineland area, doing everything from painting basement walls to laying kitchen tiles," he notes.

"Then a year later, at age 19, I went into business as a subcontractor working for the same contractor," he adds. "I had 40 people working for me, doing the labour. I was able to do the work at less cost and I doubled the money I was making."

A year later, Reimer had just turned 20 when he decided to become a full-fledged contractor and built a large house in Grimsby on speculation that once it was built, he'd find a buyer. In fact, a doctor and his new bride soon purchased the luxury dwelling.

Then, Reimer built a second, move-up house for the same doctor.

Buoyed by his success, Reimer continued

building homes from Niagara Falls to Hamilton. "Our motto was to have satisfied customers – which kept us very busy," he recalls with a smile.

Building A Better Life

"When I was a kid, I never had enough money to buy an ice cream cone, and I was determined to build a better life for my children," Reimer explains.

"So I ended up working seven years straight before I ever took a vacation."

It was also in 1957, that Reimer took the fateful step of becoming a general contractor, taking over the business of a contractor who had retired.

Reimer lacked start-up capital. But he did have someone who believed in this ambitious young man. Robert Johnson, president of the Penn Cashway in Grimsby, told Reimer he was there to help if Reimer needed his assistance. "He told me if there was ever anything I needed, to contact him," Reimer recalls, "so I went to him and asked him to lend me $250,000."

"**Mr. Johnson** wrote a cheque for $250,000 and as he handed it to me, he told me it was his retirement money so if I blew it he'd have worked his whole life for nothing," Reimer recollects. "It was a big responsibility and I wasn't about to let him down. I paid him back in six months with 6 per cent interest."

Reimer went on to build many homes across Niagara and Hamilton areas, including the homes of prominent doctors and dentists; along with the Auch Mar neighbourhood on Hamilton Mountain.

Building largely in the Grimsby area, he constructed starter, move-up and retirement homes for repeat customers, who were enthralled with the quality of workmanship they had found in their starter homes.

By his early twenties, Reimer had emerged as an up-and-coming builder with a reputation for great workmanship and strict attention to details.

The fatherless war-child had risen from an impoverished start and excelled in his new homeland.

He was now in full control of his game.

But this successful young man was about to receive news that would take him by surprise.

An Overwhelming Experience

"I was 16 when we got word that my father was still alive," Reimer says, his eyes widening from the memory. "It was an overwhelming experience."

In 1962, with help from Vineland's Mennonite congregation, Anna Reimer arranged for a meeting with Russian leader **Nikita Khrushchev** during his visit that year to the United States. **Khrushchev personally intervened and in a short time, returned Peter Reimer to his family.**

Rudy Reimer was 26 when he was reunited with his father, who had spent 18 years in prison.

"I hadn't seen my dad since I was seven years old and I thought for sure he'd been killed," Reimer says, slowly shaking his head. "It was a very emotional reunion. But it was great to have my dad back after all those years apart."

The Move To Burlington

By 1961, serviced land had become scarce in the Grimsby area. But Reimer had also started several developments in Burlington, so he made another fateful move and became a highly active builder in Burlington, building the Tyandaga Estates and Ravenswood subdivisions, many North Shore homes and numerous other prestigious dwellings.

Reimer has built homes for many prominent lawyers, doctors and other professional people and executives, including the former chairman of Quebec Hydro, and a former vice-president of Ford Motor Company of Canada. In particular, Reimer built a number of executive homes in the Tyandaga area, including his own palatial home.

A 1970 open house drew 12,000 people, police crowd control and a lot of publicity.

In fact, Reimer often moves into one of his homes in the neighbourhoods he builds. He's lived in 30 houses since age 20 and he often sells his personal homes fully furnished.

His current home features a 3,000-square-foot bedroom – that's about triple the entire floor space of an average bungalow.

Going Commercial

In 1972, Reimer had already built more than 2,000 homes when he was encouraged by the City of Burlington to take on commercial development. He became so successful at this type of development that in 1975, he switched to exclusively developing office and manufacturing buildings.

One of his first, and highly successful Burlington-located commercial projects in the early 1970s was an office and warehousing building at Mainway and Blair Road.

Next was a commercial building holding the Royal Bank, on Harvester Road.

"Burlington is a real business community," Reimer smiles. "The income level here tends to be better, and many people are either businessmen or they think like businessmen. The community has a business-like approach to growth and creating success."

A Full-Service Approach

Reimer quickly emerged in Burlington as a full-service developer, acquiring raw land, servicing the site, developing, financing and promoting the development and then selling the finished product.

Simply put, he did it all. And still does. He also manages and leases out many of his various commercial complexes.

He usually likes to build for himself and then sell or lease out the space.

In fact, Reimer Construction excels at doing its own land developing, design, building, leasing and decorating.

"That's how we still like to do business," Reimer explains. "When you can do the whole thing – you can make more money down the road."

In 1989, Reimer married Teresa Mercer, a native of Georgia. Prior to getting married, the two planned their dream home and it took nearly two years to complete the magnificent 15,000-square-foot home. The bathroom alone is larger than homes he'd lived in as a child in Europe. "In my life, I've experienced the poorest of accommodations and I've experienced the best of accommodations," Reimer acknowledges, "and

I'm very grateful for the opportunity to achieve success after experiencing poverty."

In 1990, the newlywed Reimer began building the impressive office towers off Burloak Drive where the penthouse headquarters of Reimer Construction were previously located. Many buildings are sold to investors while he continues to manage the complexes.

A Major Commercial Developer

By the early 1990s, Reimer had built more than 1-million square feet of commercial space in impressive glass towers seen throughout Burlington, but especially along the Queen Elizabeth Way.

These developments include Burloak Park on the Oakville border, consisting of a seven-storey tower, a new five-storey tower and research centres. Twelve acres of this 100-acre site were sold to the Royal Bank of Canada for its Ontario headquarters.   He's also built a convention centre in the Burloak Business Park that seats 900 people.

It features three main halls and two board-rooms. Occupancy took place in 2000 and there were immediate bookings for conventions before the project was even completed.

In early 2002, Reimer completed building a modern, state-of-the-art, 11-storey, 235,000-square-foot, glass tower.

It's regarded as Burlington's most modern, energy-efficient building.

The impressive structure also houses the new headquarters of Reimer Construction. Reimer's wife Teresa's T. Reimer Design company and his son's company are also located here.

Reimer has leased out 65 per cent of the space in the newly completed office tower and has drawn major corporations – including General Electric Co. and International Truck and Engine Co. – as tenants.

Other major firms that at one time or another, made their home in a Reimer building, include: Bank of Montreal, Canadian Imperial Bank of Commerce, TD Bank, Trebor Allen, Cadbury, AIG Life, National Bank, Brinks Security; CUMIS, John Deere, London Life, the Bailey Controls company, Zenon Environmental, Shaklee Canada Ltd., ABN Ambro Bank, and Westbury International.

New Project

And there's a new project in the works. On the Reimers' return from Spain in the summer of 2002, couple brought back some more ideas that may lead to another major project. Reimer is planning to build the largest commercial complex in Burlington.

He's already dubbed the elaborate structure 'The Palace'. And he's now actively contemplating constructing the complex at a location just off South Service Road in Burlington.

The trip to Spain inspired Reimer to come up with the proposed 300,000-square-foot complex, loosely based on the Westin Palace hotel in Madrid.

He hopes to start in on construction of the project in the months ahead and may eventually move his head office to the proposed, 12-storey structure, which is to feature high ceilings, elegant columns and a soaring rooftop dome and skylight.

The new commercial complex will also hold a convention centre, which is not expected to be a competition problem for the existing business park's convention facilities as there is currently no shortage of people interested in leasing space at the facilities for an array of upcoming scheduled events.

Although hard work is an important part of Reimer's success strategy, it's only one component.

"I've seen many hard-working people who are very poor," he says.

"It's important not just to work hard, but to work smart as well, to cut unnecessary costs and add value to really please your customers."

"If you can find ways to work smart and make your customers happy, you'll get referrals and repeat business that are going to make you successful today, tomorrow and well into the future."

Attributes Success To Others

Reimer attributes his company's enduring success to his staff, his investors, his tenants and the people who have believed in him and supported his career in one way or another over the years.

"I think one of the reasons we have been successful is that we always try to exceed the **expectations of our investors,** our tenants and everyone else who does business with us," he asserts.

"People don't realize how easy it is to make money – all you have to do is satisfy your customer."

Rudy Reimer's tips for success:

1. Behave ethically and honestly at all times. Treat everyone fairly, as you yourself would like to be treated.

2. Do your homework when you take on a new job or business. Learn all you can about the work involved so you can increase your expertise and gain new skills.

3. Hire the best people you can find and keep them motivated and contributing their skills to your endeavours. Make sure they understand their efforts are appreciated.

4. Do as much work as you can in-house, contracting out only the most necessary tasks to experienced outside consultants.

5. Know your limitations. While you should keep most work in-house, make sure you do not go beyond your expertise. It can save money to bring in a consultant as needed.

6. Work hard – but also work smart. Hard work alone won't earn success. You should always work as efficiently as possible.

7. Learn to delegate. Part of working smarter means letting others perform routine tasks.

8. Know your market. Develop a business plan and do some research to determine who and where your customers are.

9. Provide the best value you can at a good price and deliver what you promise.

10. Make your customers happy. In addition to providing the customer good value, throw in unexpected extras that will draw a smile.

11. Network. Your customers and suppliers are good sources for putting you in touch with other potential customers through referrals.

12. Find the lowest cost, best way of providing your goods or services and pass some of the savings on to the customer, either in the form of reduced costs or enhanced value.

13. Be prepared to put in long hours while building your firm into a successful entity.

14. No matter how busy you get with business, always allow time for your loved ones – and reward yourself and your family when your business starts to succeed.

15. Make sure that whatever your business endeavour is, it's something you truly enjoy being involved with: Your work should be an enjoyable challenge – not a chore – and it should be beneficial to your community.

16. As you build your company, make sure you contribute to your community, your religion and charity as a prosperous community also makes for successful people.

Teresa Reimer

Chapter 8

Teresa Reimer

Designed To Succeed

"We include decorative columns, mirrors and woodwork to achieve an interesting and formal yet warm look. I like what can best be described as a neo-classical look using pillars and marble – it's a blend of classical and modern influences,"

- Teresa Reimer

At a Glance: Teresa Reimer
and T. Reimer Design Consultants Inc.

Teresa Reimer
Age: 40
Title: President, T. Reimer Design Consultants Inc.
Claim to fame: Performs outstanding and imaginative interior design work for clients, with most of her talent dedicated to the interiors of buildings developed by husband Rudy P. Reimer. She's the 2002-2003 President of the Junior League of Hamilton-Burlington Inc. and is a board member of the Hamilton Philharmonic Orchestra. With her husband, she supports many charities.
Financial Data: Undisclosed. Private Company.
Personal: Resides in Burlington with husband Rudy P. Reimer in a dream house the couple planned out together.
For More information:
Contact: T. Reimer Design Consultants Inc.:
(905) 336-8775
Fax: (905) 336-7936.
Address: 9th Floor, Reimer Millennium Tower, 5500 North Service Road, Burlington, Ontario, L7L 6W6.
email: treimer@sympatico.ca

Chapter 8
Teresa Reimer
Designed To Succeed

As the wife of a prominent builder, Teresa Reimer is right at home with Junior League's slogan: "Women Building Better Communities."

Teresa, president of the Junior League of Hamilton-Burlington Inc., has spent the past 14 years supporting various Junior League charitable works and improving the lives of countless people.

She also works on many charitable ventures with husband, Rudy P. Reimer. She clearly takes pride in improving the world around her.

And as the president of T. Reimer Design Consultants Inc., Teresa enjoys transforming cold corporate spaces into warm inviting places.

Visit a Reimer building and you'll find her work everywhere. An office on one floor has elegant shades of blue and a modern motif. An office on another floor features warm shades and a Romanesque influence. Everywhere there are plants and personal touches that transform office space into human space.

Teresa is also an executive on the board of the Hamilton Philharmonic Orchestra and is a member of the National Register's Who's Who of Executives and Professionals for 2003-2004. The House of Lloyd,

Canada, a Reimer tenant, recently praised her work.

But while she loves interior design work, she draws a great deal of satisfaction helping others. She's raised funds for **Joseph Brant Memorial Hospital, Theatre Aquarius and Burlington Teen Tour Band**.

"Every year, Rudy has a crusade and he's great at promoting and supporting a cause, while I like doing a lot of the behind-the-scenes work," she says from her elegant, ninth floor office in one of the newer, 11-storey, glass towers built by Reimer Construction.

"We make a great team," adds Teresa, 40, surveying the panoramic view from her office in a 235,000-square-foot building situated in the 100-acre Burloak Business Park, opposite Bronte Provincial Park at the Burlington-Oakville border.

Together with her husband, Teresa Reimer has become a positive force in the Burlington area. She has a well-earned reputation as a caring woman who has made a major difference in the community.

How this ardent Junior Leaguer came to run her own interior decorating firm, marry a prominent developer and devote her time to helping others is a story that begins in the American State of Georgia.

A Southern Belle's Story

Teresa was born in Atlanta, Georgia, the only daughter and eldest child of Inge and the late Walter Mercer. The Mercers also had a son, William, one year Teresa's junior.

After a happy childhood in Atlanta, she enrolled at Georgia State University where she majored in Marketing and earned a BBA degree.

Early into her program, she embarked on a

cruise – a high school graduation gift from her parents. It was a voyage that would forever change the life of the tall and attractive, slender, young blonde.

While wandering around the crowded cruise ship, she happened upon Rudy Reimer, a Canadian businessman busily trying his luck at the ship's many gaming tables.

"I could see he wasn't having much luck." she recalls with a grin. "He threw down some chips and asked me to play for him – he forced me to gamble."

Happy Face

"So I did play," she continues, "and I doubled his money. I gave him back his original $100 and kept the winnings and walked away. At the end of the cruise, I saw him again on the dock. I'd written him a little thank you note and drew a happy face on the note – I honestly thought I'd never see him again."

Later, he sent flowers, which prompted her to telephone her thanks. "Rudy told me years later he thought the smiley face I drew had a deeper meaning," Teresa recalls. "I find it very touching that he kept it for over 20 years. One day he pulled it out of his wallet to show it to me. He carries it like a talisman."

"It was amazing," she says. "He sent flowers every second week for ages – he spent thousands a year on flowers. I always called to thank him, but for the first few years, I only saw him twice. He talked more to my mom than me, as I wasn't home much. He'd send flowers and tape recordings he made to let me know how he was doing and what he was up to. I didn't know any guy my age that would go to such extremes, so I thought it's got to be love. He was so persistent."

She says the flowers also had the effect of chasing away any would-be suitors at the college.

"Getting those flowers every other week while I was living on campus kept the other guys away because they assumed I had a steady boyfriend – I figure now that was his strategy," she smiles.

Soul Mates

"After graduating from university I became even more interested in him. I went from just thinking he was a nice guy, to falling in love with him. I realized we're soul-mates and that this is the guy I'll spend the rest of my life with."

She moved to Burlington in 1989 and began doing interior design work for Reimer Construction, founding her own company two years later.

The couple made wedding plans and married in 1989 after first planning their 15,000-square-foot dream home together. She would later hold house tours at her own home and other large area homes to raise funds for charity. The events drew upwards of 7,000 people and raised many tens of thousands of dollars.

Dubbed 'The Plantation' the Reimer mansion near Guelph Line in Burlington has a master bedroom that boasts 3,000 square feet of space and the bathroom is a full 50-feet-long.

"Make sure you really have to use the bathroom, as it's a hike getting there," Reimer laughs.

Despite its size, Teresa has given her home a comfortable yet elegant, lived-in look.

In fact, Teresa has a proven knack for creating powerful yet warm decors that are infused with an understated opulence.

"I've always liked decorating and I found I had a knack for it," notes Teresa who was initially a salaried employee of Reimer Construction, serving as the company's in-house design consultant.

The in-house work soon led to Teresa starting her own independent firm with Reimer Construction as its biggest single customer.

"We include decorative columns, mirrors and woodwork to achieve an interesting and formal yet warm look," she explains.

Neo-Classical Look

"I like what can best be described as a neo-classical look using pillars and marble – it's a blend of classical and modern influences," she adds.

Although she occasionally performs contract work outside of Reimer Construction, most of Teresa Reimer's interior design work remains focused on the prestige commercial complexes owned and/or managed by her husband.

"It's more than enough to keep me very busy," Teresa says with a laugh. "After all, we've got more than a million square feet of space to see to in 20 buildings with 110 tenants. And there are often new tenants moving into our buildings."

"I also enjoy listening to our tenants and helping them out by meeting their needs," she adds.

"Rudy gave me some seed money to help get me going. He provides the office space, receptionist and staff."

"My husband is the mastermind behind all of this," Teresa says, spreading her arms as if to take in all of the many commercial complexes that comprise

Reimer Country. In fact, Teresa is known for having the most innovative, state-of-the-art design work on the market and has completed over a million square feet of interiors. She also manages the operating costs related design for nine buildings.

"Rudy is the entrepreneur with the vision," she adds. "He's very energetic. He's certainly got more energy than I do. When he sets his mind on something, there's no stopping him. Rudy will never retire because he loves doing business deals, and he's very gutsy – I admire that about him."

Bringing Out The Best In Each Other

Teresa says she and her husband bring out the best in each other "and we've found that we're perfectly matched for each other – we really do make a great team. A lot of people won't believe this, but Rudy used to be shy – but I brought that out of him."

"I make him young – and he ages me," she says, suppressing a giggle. "Life with Rudy is a labour of love – with an emphasis on the labour," she adds with a snicker.

All joking aside, Teresa describes her marriage as "really, really great," adding that life with the dynamic developer has also meant meeting many celebrated world figures, including former U.S. President Bill Clinton, who struck her as "charming, charismatic, graceful and brilliant," former Prime Minister Brian Mulroney and wife Mila and the late Queen Mother.

Teresa enjoys making travel arrangements on behalf of herself and her husband – "I plan it out and look after all the details" – and the couple enjoys spending two to three months a year visiting other

190

countries. To keep memories of the trips fresh and alive, Teresa takes numerous photographs and keeps extensive photo albums and scrapbooks.

"I love the butterfly garden in Singapore," she says. "We've also gone to Africa, Australia and Spain. We love travelling. Rudy picks up ideas about building and I sometimes come away with some design ideas."

Dedicated To The Junior League

Teresa estimates spending 50 hours a week on her business and another 20 hours per week on Junior League.

During her first two years with the Junior League, Teresa sat on the design committee for Ronald McDonald House in Hamilton and helped raise $250,000 in gifts-in-kind.

The Junior League is currently focused on a capital campaign for Grace Haven, a centre for pregnant adolescents, women and young single parents. Programs are available on a residential and community basis. Services include a high school program, clothing exchange, parenting skills development, counselling and life skills training.

"In my 11 years with the Junior League of Hamilton-Burlington, we've distributed more than $490,000 to our local communities," Reimer notes. "These purposeful grants and disbursements allow our organization to make a positive difference."

Founded a century ago in the United States, the Junior League organization now boasts 296 League groups in 45 countries. There are eight leagues in Canada. In addition to Hamilton-Burlington – which has 200 members – locations include Montreal, Halifax, Toronto, Calgary, Edmonton, Winnipeg and Vancouver. All Canadian leagues are affiliated with the entire U.S.-based organization. Reimer says her involvement with Junior League has helped her develop and hone organizational/ managerial skills.

"The women in the league amaze me with their dedication, commitment and enthusiasm, along with the skills they bring to the process," Reimer smiles.

Giving Back

For eight years straight, Reimer also put on puppet shows with four-foot-tall puppets to teach children at dozens of schools about social issues such as vandalism. Puppet skits were also used to increase awareness of disabilities, including asthma, leukemia, diabetes, blindness, deafness and cerebral palsy.

"Another nice thing about my Junior League involvement is that I've met so many interesting, talented and inspiring women," Reimer notes.

Junior League has approximately 192,000 female members worldwide. The League was established to give women the opportunity to contribute their skill sets to worthy causes. Among the League's prominent former members is Laura Bush, wife of U.S. President George W. Bush.

"Basically we draw from the talents of successful women who volunteer their expertise – in anything from accounting to legal work or artistic or marketing skills – to projects we elect to support," Reimer explains.

"Junior League participation is a great way to give back to your community," she adds. "There's a lot of satisfaction in helping others."

Teresa Reimer's tips for success:

1. Play to your strengths. Find something that you like doing and that you're **good** at doing – then excel in this endeavour.

2. Form alliances with others (Eg: Junior League) as this can bring added skills into the equation.

3. Be prepared to put in **long hours**. But invest your time wisely to achieve your goals.

4. Learn not only to develop your own talents but also those of others. Try to bring out the best in yourself and everyone around you.

5. Go beyond merely satisfying your customer. Delight your clients by going the extra mile to deliver **impressive added touches**.

6. Support charities and worthy causes. You can make a difference. Giving back to your community can be very satisfying.

7. Praise staff for good work. This rewards and encourages more great performances.

8. **Organize your time**. There's a lot you can achieve if you focus on the important tasks at hand and not become distracted.

9. **Listen to your customers**. Find out what they want and try to meet their needs.

10. Do business in an **honest and forthright manner** – and grow through many referrals.

Rudy K. Reimer

Chapter 9

Rudy K. Reimer

The New Generation

"My father will often come up with a concept and design and he'll do a feasibility study. Then, I'll fine tune the design and make sure it's cost-effective and that the layout is functional. I'll improve the design if necessary and build the best project possible... If we build it, they will come."

- Rudy K. Reimer

At a Glance: Rudy K. Reimer and R. K. Reimer Developments:

Rudy K. Reimer

Age: 45

Title: President R. K. Reimer Developments Limited.

Claim to fame: Major developer of commercial buildings. Tenants read like a Who's Who of International business leaders. With his father, Rudy Reimer Sr., he's changing Burlington's skyline and turning the city into a major commercial centre.

Personal: Resides in Burlington with wife Jan and daughter Brittany. He's the only son of Rudy Reimer Sr. and has a sister, Darlene. He's also a private pilot who enjoys flying and traveling.

For More information:

Contact: R. K. Reimer Developments Limited: (905) 336-8775

Fax: (905) 336-7936.

Address: 9th Floor, Reimer Millennium Tower, 5500 North Service Road, Burlington, Ontario, L7L 6W6.

Email: rkreimer@sympatico.ca

Chapter 9

Rudy K. Reimer

The New Generation

Rudy K. Reimer is part of a bold new generation of builders with a confident outlook on the future: **"If we build it, they will come,"** he says with a smile.

"That's our philosophy," adds the president of R. K. Reimer Developments Limited as he surveys an impressive view of glass towers at Burloak Park in the heart of Reimer Country.

And it seems that whatever Reimer builds, there are plenty of prospective tenants eager to move into his impressive commercial buildings.

It helps that he knows all the angles.

"I don't think we've ever built a true square building – they're all asymmetrical in design," notes Reimer, 44, gazing through an angled window at a panoramic view of Burlington, Hamilton, Lake Ontario and the Niagara Escarpment.

"The more angles you have, the more views you can have," he explains. "It makes for a more conversational architecture. A square building only has four corners per floor for the executive suites, whereas an irregular shape provides for many more."

Indeed, Reimer and his company are known for the exacting standards they apply to building construction.

Lasers are routinely used to establish precise angles and total accuracy in the buildings, which are always designed to feature a number of angles and afford many great views.

Reimer established his company in 1979 and it has gone on to achieve considerable success in the ensuing decades.

The company does projects on behalf of Reimer Construction along with its own projects. It also does all of the property management for all the Reimer buildings.

Successful Company

"We'll keep on moving forward – we've got a good thing going – my staff and our trades people are behind us, helping us earn respect," he notes.

"We sell our buildings or turn over the management to others – providing we're confident the tenants will receive an equal level of quality in property management that would be to industry standards," Reimer notes.

"Our property management portfolio is something we don't want to contract out as we could lose the personal touch we provide," Reimer points out.

"Our success has been built on the personal contact and services we give to our tenants. Our goal is leasing space – still the most profitable – but the management side is still very important to us and it always will be."

Reimer says tenants have come to appreciate the company's hands-on approach and willingness to make leased space feel like home.

"The personal touch we provide has helped fuel the company's growth – and I enjoy the work. It's fun building. Every day it's something new. We're changing the landscape, building something new. It's a great way to get some fresh air in the summer, and stay warm inside during the winter."

In addition to building, Reimer, a private pilot, also enjoys flying every chance he gets. He also enjoys landscaping, spending time with his young daughter, astronomy and evenings out with friends.

Studies market conditions

Before a building project is undertaken, the company studies market conditions and determines the project's feasibility and likelihood, in the given environment, of attracting enough 'triple-A' tenants.

If conditions are viewed as favourable by his company's standards, the company will build the structure and then lease out the space, and manage the property.

"Our standard of a good economic climate is different than others," Reimer states. "We have always found it better to construct in a poor economy rather than a robust season."

Reimer's key role – one he excels at – is to add value to concepts his father envisions and then help make each project a reality by taking a very practical, cost-efficient approach to construction.

"My father will often come up with a concept and design and he'll do a feasibility study and give me a rough sketch of what he has in mind," Reimer explains.

"Then, I'll fine tune the design and make sure it's cost-effective and that the layout is functional and is workable in terms of building codes, fire codes and zoning," he adds.

Savings reinvested in improvements

"I'll improve the practicality on paper, if necessary, then we'll finally bring in our architect to add the final touches," Reimer says, noting that limiting the architect's contracted involvement in the overall process can generate substantial cost savings, which can be transferred on to other building improvements, giving tenants superb space at highly competitive rates.

"By the time we go to the architect, the concept is fully in place – and it's all been done in house. We've already priced the building and completed our budget."

"We pre-plan but avoid any excessive over-planning. We get involved with our trades people on a regular basis and co-ordinate their input and expertise.

We're constantly learning new ways to improve efficiencies," he adds.

"The bottom line is: We have the expertise to build in the most economical and safest manner possible – and we'll build the **best project possible**," Reimer asserts.

"We know what we want and our approach streamlines the whole process without cutting any corners. We'll more than meet all codes, standards and building guidelines."

Reimer admits the company's approach is "a little unique in our methodology – we tend to do our fine-tuning first, and the bulk of construction, last. This is unorthodox to most methods, but it helps us to eliminate additional expenditures up front, rather than later."

"It's the way we've always done business and it's worked well for us – we continue to be successful in the projects we take on, and I see this pattern continuing for some time to come," he adds.

Skilled Trades Shortage Concern

However, one concern Reimer sees on the looming construction horizon is a coming shortage of young skilled trades people to replace the older generation.

"Most of our trades men are middle-aged and older," Reimer notes, "and there really isn't anyone out there to replace them."

"What we're always looking for are skilled trades people who will have the necessary skills and pride in their work to satisfactorily replace the highly skilled and dedicated older trades people we have now," he asserts.

"Unfortunately, the trades usually aren't a young person's first choice for an occupation – but there's no good reason for that. These are good, well-paying jobs that need to be filled," he adds.

"The days are long gone when we could look to immigrants from Europe to fill those skilled trades jobs. The post-war boom to "make a new life in America," and the ethnical Baby Boomers associated with it, have subsided substantially."

Reimer says today's youth should seriously consider skilled trades work as a satisfying and well-paying way to make a living.

A new generation of skilled workers is also essential to propel successful companies forward.

Says Reimer: "If you don't have a highly skilled workforce, you can't compete."

Born To Build

And Reimer knows what it means to **embrace the** construction industry at a young age.

Although he was born the son of a successful developer, there were still no shortcuts for Rudy K. Reimer.

In fact, his rise to success literally began at ground level.

"I started out in the construction business pushing a **broom** during summers and after school," Reimer recalls with a smile. "I was about nine years old and being a little guy, I was just the right size for sweeping out low-headroom crawl spaces in the homes my dad built."

"Then I graduated to cleaning out whole houses – I still hold the record for the most homes cleaned in one day," he chuckles.

"When I got a little older, I was paid $6-a-lawn to cut the grass at my father's housing developments."

"Then I realized I could make better use of my time and still make a buck so I subcontracted the work out and paid my friends $3-a-lawn."

That may have been the first entrepreneurial spark from Reimer. But it wouldn't be the last from a developer who has achieved an enviable degree of success on his own.

His firm is completely independent of Reimer Construction and has earned a reputation as a leading developer.

Attention To Detail

Indeed, strict attention to details and a desire to add value and exceed expectations are common threads tying Rudy K. Reimer's company and the various Reimer Country companies together.

With such laudable shared values in place, these independent companies are well positioned to take on and conquer any and all challenges they may encounter as we move ever deeper into the new millennium.

As a youngster growing up in Burlington, Rudy K. Reimer had the advantage of being more focused than most of his peers.

"I always knew I'd be in the family business and I tended to concentrate more on that than on my schoolwork at times," he recalls.

"At age ten, I would reproduce front and rear elevations of our homes from the 'sight-to-paper' method, with good accuracy," he adds.

"By Grade 12, I knew a lot more about **framing houses** than math. But this is a constant learning experience and I later became good at math because I use it in building."

Gateway To Burlington

And he does a lot of building. The newest project on stream is a 300,000-square-foot office complex complete with retail space and a new convention centre, planned for a South Service Road location.

"This is the business hub for all of Burlington, it's its own commercial centre, also known as Reimer Country," he states.

"We now have well over 100 major tenants here, including the Burlington Convention Centre, which act as magnets for bringing other business people to this area," he notes.

"This area has become a catalyst for growth and has helped fuel the city's infrastructure potential," he adds.

"We continue to believe that Burlington is the place to be – and we're proud to be playing a role in the city's development as a major commercial centre."

Rudy K. Reimer's tips for success:

1. Always set a **goal** for yourself, whether it's profit oriented, or otherwise. It's important that you should always try to do whatever it is you like to do.

2. Be efficient with your time. Time is of the essence – use it wisely.

3. Try to excel in school. You may not like certain subjects – such as math – but you may need these subjects in the working world.

4. Respect your employees and people you work with. You can't do everything by yourself. You'll need the help of other people, so treat them well.

5. Learn to delegate. It makes more sense to assign day-to-day tasks to others to free up your time. Time is of the essence.

6. Build, and maintain, a personal touch with clients. Nurturing a business relationship can mean repeat business and referrals that will help your company grow.

7. Take pride in your work. If you're pleased with the job you've done, others will feel the same way.

8. Treat your business as a constant learning experience. Never accept that you know it all, because you don't. Build your knowledge base.

9. Enjoy what you do. Your business should also be your hobby. When it's no longer fun to do, it just becomes work. Once it's just work, it's only a job. To remain motivated and be successful, you should derive a sense of satisfaction from your work.

10. Be persistent and assertive and **always do** what you say you're going to do. Don't be intimidated by anyone. You should always believe you're as good or better than the other guy. Have **confidence in yourself** and don't put yourself down.

Closing Notes:
Through Fields of Gold

Much like the first volume, this book –
Winning Ways Vol. 2, More of the Right Stuff –
has again taken us on another remarkable journey
through the fields of success.

As we've learned from the many successful
people profiled in this book, the fields of success are far
from level or lined with convenient paths. In fact, these
fields are littered with obstacles.

A great deal of rough terrain, detours and
unexpected pitfalls must be conquered before one can
reach the fields of gold at the end.

Several of our exemplary subjects began life in
Italy and immigrated as children with their parents to a
new life in Canada.

But for John DiLiberto, Dr. Tony Mancuso and
Sam Mercanti, this new life wasn't exactly a cake walk.
As Italian-Canadians, they had a language barrier to
overcome.

Speaking English – something most of us take
for granted – was a skill DiLiberto, Mancuso and
Mercanti needed to acquire.

All three had also hailed from small towns and
villages in the temperate Italian countryside. Now they
had to get used to winter – real winter with snow and
freezing temperatures – in Hamilton, a major Canadian
city, with steel mills and high-rise buildings replacing

the rolling farmlands of their childhood.

And there was a new culture to acclimatize to, a culture that went deeper than hockey, Mounties and maple syrup (and some would add Canadian back bacon and beer), to include harder-to-define Canadian attitudes and ways of doing things in business and Society.

Rudy Reimer went through many of the same difficulties, including a language barrier and the new culture. He also had the truly traumatic experiences of escaping Nazi Germany, losing his father for 16 years (they were reunited only after Nikita Khrushchev had personally intervened) and then burning the midnight oil here in Canada to thoroughly educate himself in his chosen occupation in the construction industry.

Faced with such formidable obstacles, they might have considered themselves lucky to have simply caught up to the rest of us, mastered the language, adapted to the culture and climate, and gone on to eke out a modest living. But that's not what happened.

DiLiberto instead became a prominent real estate broker and appraiser and one of the top real estate agents in the entire country, selling more than $100-million in real estate over the past 15 years.

Mancuso became a prominent dentist and a mentor to other dentists.

Mercanti is doing "a bang-up job every time," as the CEO of CARSTAR Automotive Canada, the leading collision repair business in Canada with nearly $100-million in annual revenue.

Reimer has achieved success as a prominent developer of Burlington area commercial real estate.

Nor does having an existing familiarity with the

language and culture guarantee a smooth ride to the top. It seems there are always obstacles of one kind or another in the way.

Ken Lindsay took on a heavy debt-load – far heavier than he felt comfortable with – as a necessary measure to finance his mortgage broker firm and make his business dreams a reality.

Lindsay was determined to succeed so he took a calculated risk to remove a big obstacle – financing – and take his business to the next level.

Rosaleen Citron seemed to have everything going for her, including an enviable degree of business success. And she was happily riding a high-tech wave of prosperity.

Then, the dot-com bubble burst. Dot-com went dot-bust and many IT – information technology – firms went under. Once-buoyant high-tech stocks sank like stones. And many of these companies' leaders threw up their hands and quit in droves.

Not Citron.

She engineered a come-back and redefined her business to emphasize IT security. Citron then founded WhiteHat Security Inc., now a leading information technology security provider.

Each chapter on these various successful people has taken a close look at their life stories, the hardships they faced and the obstacles they overcame to eventually achieve lasting success.

Although their stories are all unique, all have some common elements: In every case the successful person was driven to succeed, whether their motivation to excel was to please themselves or to please their parents or loved ones. This inner drive is an essential element to nurture in anyone's quest for success.

I believe it was Thomas Edison who once said genius is 10 per cent inspiration and 90 per cent perspiration. That's probably about the right ration. It simply isn't enough to have a great idea, you have to work on it, develop it, market and promote it.

Many geniuses have gone nowhere because they haven't put in the hard work necessary to take their brilliant idea beyond the idea stage. Genius and talent aren't enough. Hard work is needed too.

But even hard work isn't enough. As Rudy Reimer notes, there are many hard-working people who are lucky if they make ends meet.

Hard work is laudable and necessary, but it's also important to work smart, to focus your energy in those areas that yield the biggest returns on effort. You can work very hard at being a brick-layer and never get wealthy. Or, you can work smarter in the planning and design side of the construction field and do well.

All of the people featured in this book are talented, driven, hard-working and smart-working leaders in their respective fields. Their success tips closing off their chapters provide gems of advice.

I've now compiled all of these words of advice into a series of Winning Ways Success Tips to close off this book.

While efforts have been made to consolidate all of these words into non-repeated items of advice, some repetition has inevitably occurred. But that's a good thing: A great message shared by many leaders deserves to be repeated.

Here's hoping you too achieve great success.

- Michael B. Davie.

Top 100 Winning Ways Tips To Achieve Success

1. Run don't walk when opportunity knocks, whether it is in your career or with your potential life mate. Embrace opportunity.

2. Set your goals and live by them – Follow through in everything. Pick your hero's or role models wisely and try to emulate them.

3. Don't be afraid to make mistakes, knowledge is learning what not to do.

4. Be a team player even if you are a leader – In this market lone wolves take time and energy and companies don't have the resources. Get really good at what you do and work with others to help them; it will go a long way in the near future.

5. Know something about everything and everything about something.

6. Get as many certifications as you can. These are important to your future employers and can provide a huge boost to your self esteem.

7. Do sweat the details. They're important.

8. Keep your options open: We live in an intimate global economy. Technology brings people together in seconds. Your dream job could be in Canada, the UK, South America, Australia, anywhere. Stay open to relocation as a potentially enriching opportunity.

9. Give something back: Be kind and generous to people. Be nice – you never know what will come of it.

10. Bring your dynamic energy to your business. For those just starting out, do business with a full tilt bogey, hair-on-fire attitude.

11. When you pick your life mate, soul mate, or business partner make sure you're ready to emotionally support each other in your life choices.

12. Constantly further your education. Life-long learning is essential. Most successful people never stop learning. People who stay at the top of their game will always come out ahead.

13. Be very prepared when presenting information of any kind. Attention to detail makes a difference.

14. Do your homework. Research your subject matter and make sure you become comfortably knowledgeable in your chosen area or field.

15. Make your marketing efforts aggressive, high energy campaigns that draw attention and get results.

16. Don't reinvent the wheel. Borrow great ideas that work and make them your own.

17. Learn from others. Experience and expertise of those around you is a rich resource.

18. Concentrate on the job at hand. Focus on one task at a time to achieve success.

19. Consider a wide array of options and every opportunity. Don't limit your horizons.

20. Keep your customers informed and involved so they work with you to achieve a common goal.

21. Believe in life-long learning. Try to constantly increase your education and improve yourself.

22. Support your community in any way you can. It's important to give back to society.

23. If you truly want to master something, teach it. To teach it, you must first fully understand it so thoroughly that you can instruct others.

24. Develop goals based on something you're good at and that you enjoy doing. Play to your strengths.

25. Think about what you want to achieve and set about making your dreams a reality.

26. Be fully rounded. Excel in academics, but don't be a bookworm – get involved in sports or a physical activity and develop a social life for good mental and physical health.

27. Be firm in principle but flexible in practice. For example be firm that a task must be done, but flexible as to how it's done.

28. There's no substitute for hard work. Do your work with passion and enthusiasm to succeed.

29. Embrace life-long learning and the joy of always expanding your knowledge base.

30. Delegate: You can't do everything so focus on what you're best at and bring in experts to do the rest. Surround yourself with good people.

31. Play hard and work hard. The more you put into life, the more you'll get out.

32. Practice what you preach. Set an example for others. If you don't believe in yourself, how can you expect others to believe in you?

33. Don't reinvent the wheel. It's faster to copy perfection, learn the lessons of others and make them your own. Take an expert's approach and modify it to suit your own personality and objectives.

34. Change is a constant in life. Embrace change and all the opportunities and possibilities it provides for growth and improved efficiency.

35. It's one thing to do it right, it's another to do the right thing. Balance your skills with ethics to ensure you deliver a treatment or service to someone that's right for them.

36. Adopt strong values and ethics and live up to the high standards you set for yourself.

37. Establish and nurture relationships with other people. People helping each other is the key to achieving success. Treat others as your would like to be treated.

38. Don't die with your dreams still in your heart – make your dreams a reality.

39. Try to be all that you can be. It means hard work but the results are well worth it.

40. Don't deny yourself the simply pleasures of family life and quality time with loved ones.

41. Take calculated risks to achieve success. There is no reward without risk.

42. Go out and achieve – give life your best shot.

43. Internalize a belief system that has confidence in your ability to conceive, believe and achieve.

44. Don't just satisfy your customers. Delight them by going the extra mile and delivering added value.

45. Believe in yourself. We are all capable of doing whatever we put our minds to.

46. Use debt as a tool to achieve the wealth that equity brings. Recognize that debt to gain an appreciating asset – such as a mortgage to buy a house – is good debt that can leave you further ahead long-term.

47. Build equity as this means building wealth. Why pay rent to a landlord when you can take on a mortgage and ownership of your own home – and your own destiny.

48. Consider renting out part of your home so that your tenants pay your mortgage for you.

49. Control debt – don't let debt control you. Even good debt can be too much of a good thing. It's important to reduce debts.

50. Think about what you want to achieve and set about making your dreams a reality.

51. If you'd like to start a business, first get experience and education in that field.

52. Do market research. Take a methodical, thorough approach to building the business.

53. Be prepared to work long and hard to earn a measure of success in your endeavour.

54. Don't be afraid to take on debt – and risk – to finance the achievement of your dreams.

55. Any risk you take on should be a calculated risk. You should be confident of success.

56. Make your money work for you. Always make sure you invest part of what you earn and build your wealth.

57. Behave ethically and honestly at all times. Treat everyone fairly, as you yourself would like to be treated.

58. Do your homework when you take on a new job or business. Learn all you can about the work involved so you can increase your expertise and gain new skills.

59. Hire the best people you can find and keep them motivated and contributing their skills to your endeavours. Make sure they understand their efforts are appreciated.

60. Do as much work as you can in-house, contracting out only the most necessary tasks to experienced outside consultants.

61. Know your limitations. While you should keep most work in-house, make sure you do not go beyond your expertise. It can save money to bring in a consultant as needed.

62. Work hard – but also work smart. Hard work alone won't earn success. You should always work as efficiently as possible.

63. Learn to delegate. Part of working smarter means letting others perform routine tasks.

64. Know your market. Develop a business plan and do some research to determine who and where your customers are.

65. Provide the best value you can at a good price and deliver what you promise.

66. Make your customers happy. In addition to providing the customer good value, throw in unexpected extras that will draw a smile.

67. Network. Your customers and suppliers are good sources for putting you in touch with other potential customers through referrals.

68. Find the lowest cost, best way of providing your goods or services and pass some of the savings on to the customer, either in the form of reduced costs or enhanced value.

69. Be prepared to put in long hours while building your firm into a successful entity.

70. No matter how busy you get with business, always allow time for your loved ones – and reward yourself and your family when your business starts to succeed.

71. Make sure that whatever your business endeavour is, it's something you truly enjoy being involved with: Your work should be an enjoyable challenge – not a chore – and it should be beneficial to your community.

72. As you build your company, make sure you contribute to your community, your religion and charity as a prosperous community also makes for successful people.

73. Play to your strengths. Find something that you like doing and that you're good at doing – then excel in this endeavour.

74. Form alliances with others (for example: Junior League) as this can bring additional skills into the equation.

75. Be prepared to put in long hours. But invest your time wisely to achieve your goals.

76. Learn not only to develop your own talents but also those of others. Try to bring out the best in yourself and everyone around you.

77. Support charities and worthy causes. You can make a difference. Giving back to your community can be very satisfying.

78. Praise staff for good work. This rewards and encourages more great performances.

79. Organize your time. There's a lot you can achieve if you focus on the important tasks at hand and not become distracted.

80. Listen to your customers. Find out what they want and try to meet their needs.

81. Do business in an honest and forthright manner – and grow through many referrals.

82. Always set a goal for yourself, whether it's profit oriented, or otherwise. It's important that you should always try to do whatever it is you like to do.

83. Be efficient with your time. Time is of the essence – use it wisely.

84. Try to excel in school. You may not like certain subjects – such as math – but you may need these subjects in the working world.

85. Influence the young people who will become the future workforce.

86. Respect your employees and people you work with. You can't do everything by yourself. You'll need the help of other people, so treat them well.

87. Learn to delegate. It makes more sense to assign day-to-day tasks to others to free up your time. Time is of the essence.

88. Build, and maintain, a personal touch with clients. Nurturing a business relationship can mean repeat business and referrals that will help your company grow.

89. Take pride in your work. If you're pleased with the job you've done, others will feel the same way.

90. Treat your business as a constant learning experience. Never accept that you know it all, because you don't. Build your knowledge base.

91. Enjoy what you do. Your business should also be your hobby. When it's no longer fun to do, it just becomes work. Once it's just work, it's only a job. To remain motivated and be successful, you should derive a sense of satisfaction from your work.

92. Be persistent and assertive and always do what you say you're going to do. Don't be intimidated by anyone. You should always believe you're as good or better than the other guy. Have confidence in yourself and don't put yourself down.

93. Get involved with Junior Achievement and other worthy organizations and causes to share the skills and expertise you've acquired with others.

94. Network with other members of the business community and education communities to learn from them.

95. Receive professional training to ensure your success in delivering a program or public speaking.

96. Share your experiences, mistakes and successes with future leaders by educating youth in the field of business.

97. Help build tomorrow's business leaders by serving as a mentor.

98. Choose others to become your own mentors as we can always learn from others.

99. Always strive to improve yourself and your performance.

100. Go the added distance to make sure you become the one to beat. Work hard and work smart to succeed at whatever you choose to do in life. Harness and nurture your inner drive to propel you forward into a successful future. You have what it takes – now make it happen.

Manor House Publishing
(905) 648-2193